E-Learning in Libraries

Best Practices

Edited by
Charles Harmon
Michael Messina

THE SCARECROW PRESS, INC.
Lanham • Toronto • Plymouth, UK
2013

Published by Scarecrow Press, Inc.
A wholly owned subsidiary of The Rowman & Littlefield Publishing Group, Inc.
4501 Forbes Boulevard, Suite 200, Lanham, Maryland 20706
www.rowman.com

10 Thornbury Road, Plymouth PL6 7PP, United Kingdom

Copyright © 2013 by Scarecrow Press, Inc.

British Library Cataloguing in Publication Information Available

Library of Congress Cataloging-in-Publication Data

E-learning in libraries : best practices / Edited by Charles Harmon, Michael Messina.
    pages cm
  Includes bibliographical references and index.
  ISBN 978-0-8108-8750-3 (pbk. : alk. paper) — ISBN 978-0-8108-8751-0 (ebook)
(print) 1. Libraries and distance education. 2. Internet in education. 3. Electronic information resource literacy—Web-based instruction. 4. Web-based instruction.
I. Harmon, Charles, 1960– editor of compilation. II. Messina, Michael, editor of compilation.
  Z718.85E53 2013
  025.5—dc23
                                                        2012043420

∞™ The paper used in this publication meets the minimum requirements of American National Standard for Information Sciences—Permanence of Paper for Printed Library Materials, ANSI/NISO Z39.48-1992. Printed in the United States of America.

Contents

Introduction: E-Learning and Libraries—Not Your Father's Oldsmobile

LINDA W. BRAUN
Consultant, Librarians and Educators Online

E-learning. What is that?

- Does it mean taking part in a synchronous, structured class to learn about a specific topic? Yes, it does.
- Does it mean taking part in an asynchronous learning experience where students can learn content at their own pace? Yes, it does.
- Does it mean watching and commenting on videos posted online? Yes, it does.
- Does it mean interacting with a learning community via discussion boards, blogs, Twitter, Facebook, and other forms of social media? Yes, it does.
- Does it mean accessing a curated list of resources? Yes, it does.

You get the idea. There is no one-size-fits-all for e-learning. It's a form of learning that encompasses a wide variety of technologies and experiences. In a library, e-learning can take on any of the forms and formats cited, and some e-learning experiences combine all of the above. Developing good e-learning offerings for a library means knowing the community, knowing the technology available, and being able to make the right connections between community and technology. The same e-learning experience will not work for every set of goals or for every audience.

In *E-Learning in Libraries: Best Practices*, you'll learn from those who have had practical experience with library-based e-learning, and you'll get an idea of what will work best for your community. You might decide to mix and match, using practices covered in one example with practices from another to create the best experience for those with whom you work.

WHY E-LEARNING?

Consider libraries of just a generation ago. Learning had to take place in real time and only with those who could get to the library building (or to a classroom or community space in which library staff spent time). While audio and video have been a part of library reference and circulating collections for decades, a majority of content, until recently, was available in only text-based form. While interlibrary loan was possible (and of course still is), the barriers—including the time necessary to receive loaned items—limited its use.

Today, libraries provide e-learning opportunities throughout the community. Those who come to the library can participate, but so too can those who might only use library services remotely. Video, audio, and interactive multimedia make it possible to meet the needs of different types of learners.

No longer is it up to library staff members to be the experts on all topics.

E-learning incorporates resources from the expansive set of resources available via services such as YouTube, which includes curated content of primary source materials from the Smithsonian, the Library of Congress, federal government agencies, and National Geographic, to name a few.

WHAT DOES E-LEARNING LOOK LIKE?

Here are just a few ways in which libraries can and do provide e-learning opportunities to their customers:

- A library of any type can fairly quickly develop a catalog of screencasts that support a variety of learning needs in the community—from an overview of how to use the library's e-book tools to how to use a database to support a college course; or, if a library is looking for ways to better support those new to technology, there could be screencasts that focus on computer basics.
- Have you noticed how filled with do-it-yourself and how-to information YouTube is? Have you noticed that if you search YouTube, you can find a variety of videos that explain everything from a historic event to how the Internet works? There is a reason for this wealth of videos. It's a great format for teaching and learning. A library's e-learning portfolio might include video interviews with experts or videos of lectures or programs sponsored by the library. These videos can be tagged and hosted on YouTube, added to a playlist titled with the learning topic, and made available to the community.

- Webinars on a topic of interest to community members could include experts in a field talking with participants, recorded and archived for a later viewing by those who didn't get a chance to attend live or for a later replay and review of the topic.
- Podcasts are also an effective way to develop a body of information on a variety of topics. A library staff member might interview a community member with expertise on a subject of local interest. Or library staff might produce podcasts as a form of professional development to inform others about current trends and best practices.
- Pathfinders using contemporary tools such as LibGuides may not seem like e-learning, but they are. These teach content while teaching about how to be a successful researcher.
- The library might sponsor discussions on a course topic or a topic of community interest using Twitter and a hashtag so that all the postings can be easily accessed and read together. Or, a discussion might be hosted using a traditional blogging platform, including links to resources, with questions ripe for discussion via the commenting feature of the software.

Learners involved in a library's e-learning offerings get to take advantage of all these options, too. They can demonstrate their understanding of a topic by creating and then posting content of their own in video, audio, or text format. These might include screencasts in which students/participants teach how to use databases or the library catalog; they might also include pathfinders created by learners to demonstrate their grasp of a topic they learned via an e-learning experience provided by the library.

Depending on the audience and purpose, the library might mix a variety of these components into a more formal and long-term learning experience. This might be a multiweek course using a learning management program such as Moodle as the platform for organizing and providing the various pieces of content—podcasts, screencasts, discussions, and so on.

FORMAL AND INFORMAL ARE BOTH OK

A webinar, in which an expert lectures on a particular topic, can be a useful and popular, but an informal experience could be just as valuable—specifically in which a community member starts a discussion on a library's Tumblr about a local concern and other members of the community are encouraged to react, discuss, and learn. The audience and purpose of your e-learning experience will help you to determine which style of presentation of learning you take—formal or informal.

AUDIENCE AND PURPOSE

You may have noticed that I've frequently mentioned audience and purpose in the paragraphs so far. When you build your physical library collection, it's imperative to understand for whom you are building it and what their needs are; the same is true for the e-learning resources that you offer your library's customers. Who is the audience for that e-learning? K–12 students, students in higher education, teachers and faculty in schools and academic settings? Maybe you want to reach people who never walk through the library's doors. Or, maybe you want to connect with parents who are too busy to take advantage of what the library has to offer on-site.

As you read through this volume think about the audience and purpose (or audiences and purposes) that you want to meet and achieve with the e-learning you provide. Which best practices are going to fit your immediate audience and goals? Which might be something to work toward as your audience and you become more e-learning savvy?

If you keep audience and purpose in mind from the beginning of your e-learning development, your chances of success will expand. Knowing who and why from the start will help you make decisions about format and evaluate success or failure more honestly and usefully. You'll be able to answer important questions: Did your e-learning succeed for the audience and purpose that you selected? If not, why not? If so, how? A clear focus can help you eliminate mistakes the next time—or improve on what you already did well.

WHO CAN DO IT?

Academic and school libraries might seem like the only type of libraries that this type of initiative is right for, but I'm here to tell you that e-learning is something that all libraries should integrate into their services. All libraries are a part of the educational infrastructure of the community. As you read the best practices presented in this book, consider how the same type of learning experience might be adapted for your audience and purpose, even if your library isn't the type described.

If you are new to e-learning, try out some e-opportunities yourself to get a sense of what works and what doesn't. It's not that hard to do. Many national, state, and regional library associations sponsor e-learning. Sign up for one, two, or three types of learning opportunities to understand how they work, what you have to do to get something similar started, and what would be best for your community.

E-LEARNING IN LIBRARIES: LOTS TO LOOK FORWARD TO

Because the variety of e-learning opportunities and possibilities is extremely varied, this volume can make your life much easier. In it, you will learn from others who have already taken the plunge and integrated e-learning into their libraries. You'll find out what works and what doesn't. And you'll get some ideas about what is best to try in your own library. You don't have to reinvent the wheel. You can read this book and say to yourself, "For our community, I think we should try this program that is focused on screencasts." Or, you might think, "The people to whom we provide service would benefit from a focused e-course on using library databases like the one I've just read about." Or, you might realize that you are already integrating e-learning by providing your community with remote access to carefully curated resources and that it's time you advertise them as e-learning. And if you determine that you are already providing e-learning but didn't realize it, start looking at how you can expand to support more members of the community.

The nine best practices featured in the following pages will definitely give you a lot of the information and inspiration you need.

1

Introducing Online Credit-Based Instruction for Undergraduates

LAUREN PRESSLEY
Wake Forest University Library

Wake Forest University was introduced to online undergraduate education by two sections of the library's credit-based class "Accessing Information in the 21st Century," or LIB100 as we call it. The library's dean, Lynn Sutton, and I decided to offer an online version of our credit-based information literacy class in the summer of 2011. We wanted to move quickly to make this offering, so the course was launched in the second half of the fall 2011 semester.

We believed that it was important to offer this class online for a number of reasons. For one, we believe that online education is going to greatly affect higher education, and to understand that potential impact, we needed to explore it. For another, our mission is to help our students, faculty, and staff succeed. We offer several sections of a one-credit research-based class each semester to help our students succeed in doing college-level research and to help faculty with students who can complete research projects that are easier to grade. We thought that we would extend our support of students by opening it up online to allow students to continue earning college credits in case they have a medical emergency, a family illness, a travel-abroad opportunity, or an internship scheduled for a semester in which they cannot fall behind. The library faculty have a large number of librarians who earned all or part of their masters of library science online, so the idea of online education is not controversial to the library. With this background, we decided to pursue it.

THE AIMS AND OBJECTIVES OF LIB100 ONLINE

Officially, at the time of the pilot, the class aimed to meet the following learning objectives:

By the end of this class students will be able to
  1. Determine a research question, project scope, and research strategy for research assignments.
  2. Compare and contrast reference sources, books, databases, journals, and articles.
  3. Make a well-reasoned judgment on the quality of a website for research.
  4. Use Zotero to organize bibliographic records, parenthetically cite sources, and generate bibliographies.
  5. Identify major themes in the evolution of the Internet, and identify potential trends the emerging information environment.

Unofficially, this course aimed to introduce online learning to the college, as it was the first undergraduate course taught online at Wake Forest University. I sought to create a specific instance of a high-quality Wake Forest University–style class in an online environment to illustrate that education in the "Wake Forest way" could be done online as well as in person.

TAKING THE ONLINE SECTION FROM IDEA TO REALITY

The Context

The foundation for this course was an enthusiastically supportive library administration and a teaching librarian with training in instructional design and instructional technology. Since I had taught most of my classes using a blended framework—making extensive use of tools such as various course management systems, blogs, wikis, Google Docs, and the like—it was not hard to think about shifting all the instruction to an online environment.

Due to this background, the more important issue to us was ensuring that the students who participated in the pilot understood what they were getting themselves into and what support would be available to them. As students signed up for the course, I sent them an e-mail explaining that the course would take place asynchronously online and briefly describing what successful participation would look like. I reassured them that I would be available to work with them as they came across challenges, and I also gave them an out, guaranteeing them a spot in another section of the same class if they did not feel comfortable taking the course online. A few freshmen did choose a face-to-face section instead, but most students chose to stay in the class. In fact, as registration took place, a few students signed up because they had heard that the class was online and they needed another hour but could not find anything that fit in their schedule. And this happened without any marketing on our part at all.

Designing the Course

In the month and a half leading up to the course, I undertook an extensive analysis in the instructional design of the course. I recognized that development, implementation, and evaluation would happen throughout the class as I got a sense of what worked for the students and what needed to be rethought. The analysis phase included learning the academic year of the students in the class, consulting with other librarians to find what they considered to be core to the class, and discussing with various faculty at my institution what "Wake Forest education" should look like. These faculty discussions were critical to understand what aspects to maintain in the online environment. During this phase, I also explored tools that might be useful in the online environment, and I determined those that would provide a seamless experience. The findings included a group of students who had varied exposure to the library, from freshmen to seniors about to go to graduate school. Most faculty felt that our particular style of education is about the relationship and personalized attention that students got in the classroom. Most of the students had never considered online education, in fact choosing to attend Wake Forest University because of its emphasis on face-to-face relationships with faculty. However, those who took the class were interested in experiencing online education for the sake of trying it, for the purpose of learning how it worked for graduate school, or because it enabled them to fit the course into their schedule.

With this background, the design phase was simple. I focused my energy on creating a solid and rigorous curriculum that emphasized building a relationship between students and instructor. I also built many safety valves into the course so that if students got offtrack or behind due to lack of experience as online students, they would not be penalized too harshly.

Since I knew that this course would be the case example in our campus discussions that would be analyzed across campus, I built evaluation into every step of the course. I conducted entry surveys for each unit so that I could understand the students' backgrounds. I built each unit to require "class activities" as well as the traditional out-of-class assessments. Furthermore, at the end of each class session, students were asked to create a short video summarizing the main points they took away from each unit and to tie those points to their larger studies. Having these data from each student along the way helped me to target the materials I was designing as we went and to provide personalized feedback when students were confused on specific issues.

The Tools

At the point in which I offered this class, the campus had just switched from Blackboard to Sakai for its course management system. Since students were not familiar with Sakai yet and our implementation was new enough that we had not rolled out all the features associated with the platform, I did not feel wedded to the campus choice.

With this freedom, I explored a number of options, finally setting on using a selection of products from the Google Apps suite, as well as introducing screencasting using Camtasia's Jing. With a structured front page using Google Sites (see Figure 1.1), students could navigate through course content and to their own pages by bookmarking just one website. Furthermore, I could embed several pieces of content in the one page, allowing students to

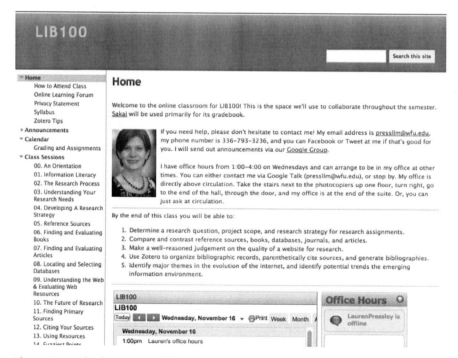

Figure 1.1. The front page of the course. Note that "Class Sessions" are listed on the left side of the page.

bookmark one site and have access to all the course content from one location. The tools embedded in the site included

- short video lectures created for the course from YouTube,
- screencasts demonstrating technical skills recorded with Jing,
- forms from Google Docs to assess the students' backgrounds,
- documents from Google Docs to allow me to update the syllabus and assignments from one central location,
- supplemental images and slide decks uploaded to Google Docs, and
- an embedded Google Calendar that allowed all deadlines and office hours to show up on my calendar and the calendars of students who subscribed to it.

This embedding was really the power of the course website. As the instructor, I juggled lots of websites and services, but the students had just one location to go to, which included everything. In fact, some of the students who enthusiastically embraced the course started embedding their own content in their personal pages on the site.

Knowing that this was an entirely new experience for everyone, I strongly recommended an orientation for the course. Students could choose to come to an in-person orientation or take one in the course itself. Most did take part in the orientation, but the in-person session was far more about the logistics of deadlines than technically how to work with the course material.

The Money and Time It Took to Conduct the Pilot

At its start, this course did not require any additional funding. We used freely available web-based technologies and the capabilities of my laptop (which included a video camera). Students at Wake Forest University are provided with laptops, so I was familiar the technological capabilities of their computers and that students did not have to purchase anything to participate. As class progressed, it became necessary to obtain additional funding for a pro account for screencasting.com. This was due to the high volume and traffic that the streaming account received as the course progressed. Had I made use of a local streaming option for this functionality, that cost would have been negated.

The biggest resource consumed by this class was time. I was given permission to defer some of my duties while developing and teaching this class; however, during that same semester, I also taught an in-person section during the first half of the semester, as I typically do, and an additional two sections the second half. The two second-half-of-the-semester sections were both held online as the pilot. The time commitment for developing the course design, creating the content, interacting with students, and grading their work cannot be overstated. However, with a longer implementation timeline, it would have been a less intense process. We knew we were committing to a significantly time-consuming project when we chose to fast-track the course.

LIB100 ONLINE IN THE LARGER UNIVERSITY CONTEXT

Our library is very focused on our mission: "to help students, faculty, and staff succeed." Our class directly supports the mission, as the research skills learned in LIB100 help in all student research projects. As stated earlier, we saw the online class as another way to help our students, who have any of a variety of reasons for needing to earn a credit when away.

Students who enrolled in the online class tended to be excited about it or at least happy that they could fit it in their schedule. However, many were a bit nervous. Over the course of the class, the reactions were very positive, and most students said that if given the opportunity to redo the semester and select this version of the class or a traditional face-to-face version of the class, they would select the online version. I know that the learning was better in this version of the class, and I was able to get to know the students better than my face-to-face students as well.

The library was supportive of this project—everyone knows that I am a passionate teacher and that I know about technology, so I do not think there was doubt about my ability to do it. Furthermore, several library faculty have online degrees, so this form of education is well received in the library community.

The college, however, was more divided. Some faculty think that online learning is important at this point in time and that we should be offering it. Others want to be very deliberative as we consider online learning and think about what that type of change might mean for the institution as a whole. Some would rather we stake our claim as a face-to-face institution. The faculty have had several discussions and forums around the issue of online learning and are taking this discussion very seriously. I was also invited to present to the College Board of Visitors, and the course received warm reception there.

As the discussions are ongoing, the library is serving as a reference for what online learning might be like. We have become a leader on campus in these issues. The larger university just hired a director of online learning to support graduate-level online courses, and the library has hired an e-learning librarian to support those graduate students as well.

No matter what happens in this discussion, the library has been a strong campus leader and will continue to be such as we offer graduate education online. Furthermore, the specific course we offered included several features that have since been adopted in face-to-face courses and blended classes at other departments within the university.

ASSESSMENT OF THE COURSE

For each session of the course, we started with a general overview of the unit. Students were told the learning outcomes and their expectations for the unit and were given a short anonymous survey. These surveys let me know how the group as a whole was starting the session, and they gave me a sense of when most of the students actually started the unit (see Figures 1.2 and 1.3).

I knew faculty at my institution would be interested in how I knew students spent time "in class," so I built in opportunities along the way to interact. These were in the form of specific questions to respond to, either personally

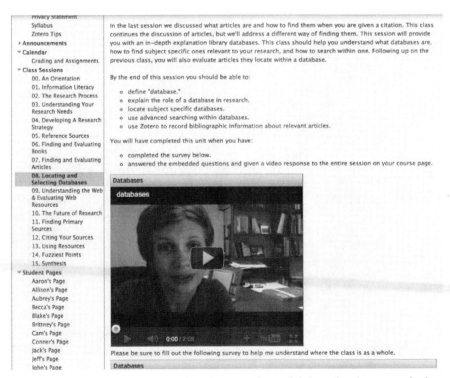

Figure 1.2. **The introductory content from a unit, explaining what is expected when students complete it.**

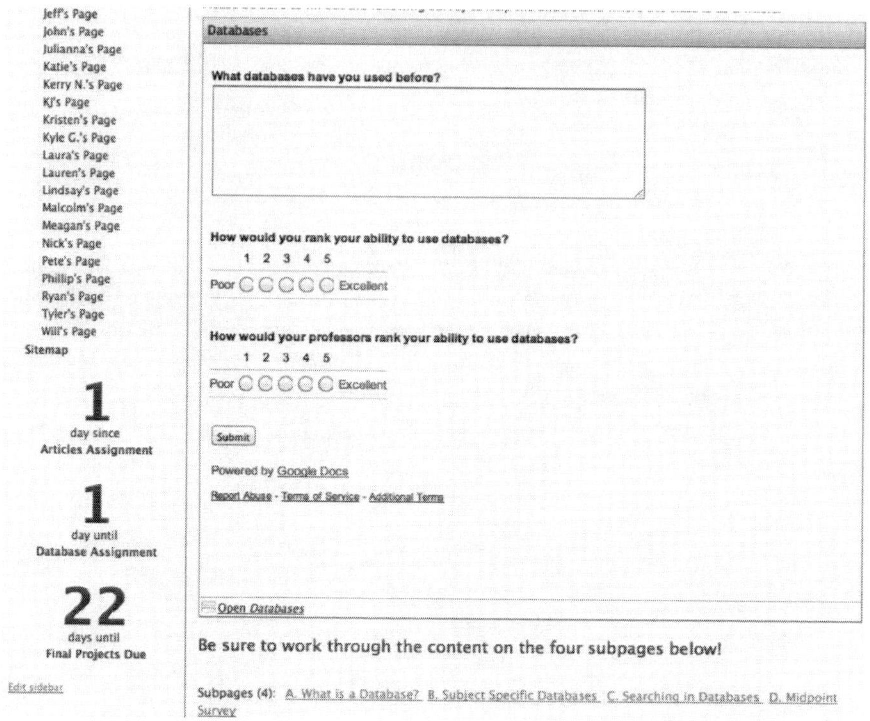

Figure 1.3. Also from the first page of the unit: a survey designed to understand prior knowledge before completion of the unit.

on their own course page or in forums with their classmates. Not only did this feedback demonstrate that the students had engaged with the content, but it also helped me see what points were clear and what needed reinforcement.

Furthermore, I knew that faculty would want to know how we could guarantee that each student actually participated. That, coupled with a focus on face-to-face relationships, led to the video requirements of the course. Students were asked to create videos after every class summarizing the main points. These videos showed me that they were engaging with the content; they helped me understand what points needed additional discussion; and they helped me get to know the students better. Seeing students in their residence hall, on the quad, or in a coffee shop talking about course content was a better foundational building block for relationships than what these discussions have been in a physical classroom in the past.

I knew that even with all the feedback that students were getting from me on their personal page posts and videos, there was still room for people to be confused and not let me know. So, I designated one class, toward the end of the semester, as the Fuzziest Points Day. Prior to that class, I had students submit three things that were still confusing, that they would like to address in more depth, and that they wished we would discuss; then, I built an entire session around those issues. The responses tended to be evenly distributed between technical issues of how to use various resources and conceptual issues of things we had mentioned briefly in class, such as augmented reality.

Up until this point, the assessments had been part of class participation. In the design of the course, both consuming course content and producing this information summed to about a typical class period. Beyond that, students had homework as they do in a face-to-face class. These assignments were built around the learning outcomes for the course to measure students' abilities to apply the principles we had covered in class. Instead of printing out the homework and bringing it to class as they traditionally do, they could either e-mail it to me or post it on their personal page.

Finally, once the course was complete, students completed evaluations. Since they knew that it was a pilot and their feedback was going to be useful to the college in discussions about online learning, most were happy to provide answers to an additional evaluation survey. Students completed the traditional evaluation for the course as well as one that I designed to target the nature of an online course. I duplicated that second survey and sent one link to the students who completed the course with minimal prompting and the duplicate out to the group that needed more support along the way. This way, we could determine if a student's predisposition to be able to take the course influenced one's perception of its success.

NEXT STEPS

The college faculty are now discussing online education for undergraduates, and as we do not want to overstep our bounds, we are waiting for their discussion to determine when we can offer the course again. However, as the place that online education has happened for undergraduates, we are taking every opportunity we can to share our story from whatever angle makes sense. In a teaching-with-technology fair, we emphasized the tools. To the College Board of Visitors, we presented findings. To faculty, we give demonstrations of the course and explain the student experience.

As the campus community continues to have discussions around online learning, the library, as a body, tries to attend discussions and offer support when it makes sense. We recently hired an e-learning librarian as well to support a new online graduate program that began in fall 2012. The library plans to be an advocate for good online education and a center of expertise for those who have questions or interest in it.

ADVICE FOR OTHERS CONSIDERING AN ONLINE COURSE

For those considering taking a course online, I cannot recommend strongly enough that you start with a consideration of what you want the student experience to be. Once you know that and have your learning outcomes, you are in a place to think about details.

At that point, I recommend that you pick a few tools that are simple but powerful rather than using every technology available to you. Initially, I scanned the environment and found many tools that would have potentially powerful educational impact. I was tempted to use them all. But with a mantra of "push button easy," I began peeling away extraneous ones until we ended up with a list of tools that we would use frequently enough to justify learning them, tools that all worked together and those with the minimal level of complexity necessary to convey the educational principles we were discussing.

Good planning saves from headaches later. Every step of this project included the thought that the content would be reused, either in future online classes or in face-to-face classes that need online supplements. This has meant (1) that other faculty in our instruction program have been able to reuse the content and (2) if we were to offer an online class again, we would be able to roll this one out with minimal changes. The time investment up front was significant, but it will realize time savings in the long run, if the class is offered enough.

I also recommend keeping this in the forefront of your thinking: Online students are students and should be treated as you treat your face-to-face ones. Yet, when you have this approach, you will note that some of the tools you will develop for your online students will be useful for face-to-face students as well and will improve the entire instruction program. A solid repository of video instruction can be useful for teaching, but it can also be useful as supplementary instruction material for one-shot sessions, for embedding in LibGuides, for embedding at the point of need throughout the website, as well as for sending in e-mail to answer reference questions.

Finally, a lesson realized in this process is that students in this class were learning to be online students while learning the course content. This meant that sometimes I was more relaxed with deadlines than I would be in my traditional class. Students have developed strategies and techniques for using face-to-face class sessions to remind them of deadlines, but they had not yet developed strategies to remind themselves of deadlines in an online environment. Students might have a hard time picking up the most important points from a collection of online text and video, whereas they have had over 12 years of training for how to learn from a lecture, so I would make points much more explicit in the online class than I would otherwise.

Even after all the work in developing the class, conducting it, providing extensive personalized feedback throughout the class, and grading assessments, I can say with confidence that this was the most rewarding class I have ever taught. I knew the students better than I have known them in my face-to-face classes, and I know that they learned more and better than students in my other classes have. The students commented that they felt close to me, and I can verify that they were more comfortable approaching me for help. The course evaluations were very positive, despite the frequent comment that it was a challenge for them to get used to fitting the work into their schedules. In fact, a number said that the course should be required, and of those comments, several said that it should be taught online. In fact, some said that because of their experience in the course, they believe that the university ought to offer more online courses.

This was a powerful experience that helped our students meet their goals and succeed. It also allowed us to position ourselves on campus to be leaders in the discussion of the future of our teaching mission as an institution, which is exactly the place where we try to be.

2

NCompass Live: Educating Nebraska's Librarians Online

CHRISTA BURNS AND MICHAEL P. SAUERS
Nebraska Library Commission

It won't be news to anyone reading this book, but library budgets are tight, and staff time is limited. As a result, many librarians can no longer travel to attend meetings and training sessions. Participation in these types of events is important for a variety of reasons. Sometimes knowledge about a particular topic is required or necessary for a librarian to do his or her job. Possibly, one needs to earn continuing education credits to receive his or her librarian certification. And, of course, the benefits of lifelong learning, in both personal lift and professional life, are well known and immeasurable.

In Nebraska, we must consider the additional issue of our population density. Most of the population lives in the far eastern part of the state, making travel to any in-person training session a hardship for many librarians. Those of us who work at the state agency for libraries and librarians do travel across the state as much as we can to provide programs and training, but it's never enough.

To help meet this need, the Nebraska Library Commission started NCompass Live, a weekly online event.[1] Yes, a webinar. An online session. A webcast. Call it what you like. What's really important is how it has increased and improved the personal professional development opportunities for librarians across Nebraska.

HISTORY

In 2008, the library commission was transitioning away from running the OCLC (Online Computer Library Center) regional network for Nebraska, NEBASE. As the OCLC member services coordinator, Christa had held monthly NEBASE Hours, webinars to keep Nebraska OCLC members up-to-date about OCLC products and services. With NEBASE closing down, these monthly webinars would no longer be offered. But the library commission still had an account with Saba Centra, the online meeting software program that had been used for NEBASE Hours. Christa realized that if we could do a monthly show just about OCLC, we could definitely do a weekly show covering all sorts of library activities! NCompass Live was born.

The name NCompass Live is based on the name of a regularly published library commission newsletter, *NCompass*. At the same time that we were developing our weekly webinar, the commission was working on the branding of our blog and podcast. To have a common brand among them, these became the NCompass Blog, the NCompass Podcast, and our weekly webinar, NCompass Live.

The purpose of the show is to inform Nebraska library staff of activities at the commission and in the library world at large. As Christa had experience with presenting online sessions, it naturally fell to her to become the organizer and host of NCompass Live. It was decided that the show would broadcast every Wednesday, at 10:00 A.M. central time. To get things started, all departments in the commission were asked to participate by suggesting topics and agreeing to present some of them. We also planned on occasionally having guest speakers from outside the commission. Given the ideas suggested by the library commission staff, Christa began contacting potential speakers.

A low-cost 5-megapixel USB web camera[2] was purchased so that video of presenters could be shown as part of the show. Today, we have upgraded to a Cannon XHA1s HD Camcorder,[3] but the original webcam is still sometimes used, depending on the availability of the larger camera. A Blue Microphones USB Snowball microphone was also purchased.[4]

These two items, a webcam and a microphone, were the only extra equipment that we needed to purchase to get NCompass Live started. At the library commission, a meeting room was used as our "studio." The room already had a desktop computer and projector installed, so we were able to use those to do our broadcast. An additional laptop computer, also already available as commission equipment, was used monitor the sessions, tracking broadcast quality and audience questions.

At the time, the library commission was participating in a group purchase of the Saba Centra software, so it was available at a discounted price. Only 6 months into the show, the library commission decided to leave the group purchase, so we needed to find a new online conferencing software program to use. The show went on hiatus for about 2 months while we investigated various options.

In the end, we choose to use GoToWebinar by Citrix.[5] It was a very simple system to use, with minimal downloading of software needed by participants.

It also works on both PC and Mac computers for live broadcasts and recordings. As the library commission is the agency for all libraries in the state, we do serve school libraries. They tend to use Macs, so it was very important to us to find a program that all of our viewers could use. The cost was also very attractive—in 2009, an annual subscription for 1,000 seats was available for $948. At the time of this writing (2012), the price has gone up, but the library commission is currently grandfathered in to our original price.

Our first two episodes of NCompass Live were used to give an introduction to the Nebraska Library Commission: "Meet the NLC, Part 1 and 2." Each department head spoke about what he or she does in one's area. Then, it was on to anything and everything library related. By our fifth episode, we had our first noncommission guest speaker, Marty Magee, from the National Network/Libraries of Medicine, to speak about free health resources from the National Library of Medicine.

During the first year of NCompass Live, Michael brought the idea to Christa about doing a monthly "techie" episode of the show. As the technology innovation librarian at the library commission, Michael saw NCompass Live as a perfect way to keep Nebraska librarians informed and aware of technology-related stories and issues. So in December 2009, the first "Tech Talk With Michael Sauers" was broadcast. Tech Talk is a monthly episode of the show, usually airing on the last week of the month but sometimes moved to the week before or after, due to scheduling changes. Starting with the 2010 Internet Librarian Conference, we have also done a live broadcast of "Tech Talk From Internet Librarian." The next year we started doing the same thing from the Computers in Libraries Conference. The conference organizers have generously worked with us to provide space and a hardwired Internet connection to do the show from the conference. We invite conference attendees to join us to share their experience at the conferences. This helps bring the national conference to our Nebraska librarians who are unable to attend the conferences in person.

HOW WE DO IT

Preproduction

Finding content for NCompass Live is the first step in putting on the show. Without our speakers, there is no NCompass Live. Christa is always keeping her eyes and ears open for show ideas. She follows library-related blogs, newsletters, and journals. Twitter, Facebook, and FriendFeed are all mined for interesting things going on at libraries across the country. She also looks through the conference agendas for our state library conference and other national conferences. We like to help presenters reach a larger audience than the in-person conference they are presenting at. As we mentioned at the beginning of this chapter, librarians everywhere are becoming more restricted in their ability to travel to conferences. By bringing conference speakers onto NCompass Live, we help these librarians participate in those conferences.

On average, Christa has 1 or 2 months of upcoming episodes scheduled. We prefer not to schedule shows out too far in advance so that if an important library issue comes up suddenly, we can get someone on the show quickly. This was the case during the SOPA/PIPA controversy in 2012. SOPA (Stop Online Piracy Act) and PIPA (Protect IP Act) were U.S. bills attempting to fight copyright infringement and online piracy, and on January 20, the House of Representatives postponed plans for both. On February 1, because we had a spot open, we were able to get Brandon Butler, from the Library Copyright Alliance, on NCompass Live to discuss the issue.

Christa contacts prospective speakers, usually via e-mail, and invites them to be on the show, letting them know what dates are open. Dates are confirmed on a first-come, first-served basis. So, follow-up e-mail is sometimes needed to let speakers know that previously available dates have been claimed.

Once a speaker has picked a date, Christa confirms if he or she will be coming to the commission to participate or joining us remotely. If one comes to the commission, she instructs the speaker to arrive approximately 15 to 20 minutes before we go live. If one is presenting remotely, she sets up a test meeting in GoToWebinar, a tech test, so that the presenter can learn how to use the system and we can test the presenter's computer and microphone. GoToWebinar uses VoIP (voice over Internet protocol) for the audio, so presenters do need a microphone if they are joining the show remotely. There is a phone number that can be used to call in, but it is a long-distance number, so we discourage both presenters and attendees from using it. During the tech test, Christa also shows the presenter how to use GoToWebinar to share their screen. The system uses simple screen sharing, not application sharing, so attendees will see anything that a presenter has on one's screen. Slides, websites, webcams, documents—anything can be shown. This also means that any presentation materials do not need to be sent to Christa ahead of time or uploaded into the system.

Christa asks the presenter to write a title and a description for one's episode. After receiving it, she schedules the episode in GoToWebinar, which generates a unique URL for logging into an episode of the show.

Then Christa adds the episode to the NCompass Live schedule via the library commission's training calendar, an in-house portal for scheduling and tracking commission trainings and events. This is where attendees can preregister for the show. The day before a show, the training calendar will automatically send a reminder message to all registered attendees, with the GoToWebinar log-in information.

When it comes to finding speakers for Michael's monthly Tech Talk episodes, it pretty much works the same as when Christa looks for all the other speakers. Michael mostly keeps his eye on library and technology blogs, Twitter streams, and Google+ for stories about interesting things being done by libraries related to technology. Michael has interviewed library leaders such as David Lee King, Sarah Houghton, and Jamie LaRue. Other topics of Tech Talks have ranged from libraries circulating GPS units, iPads, ereaders, and video games to demonstrations of the first Google laptop, library maker spaces, and LibraryThing.

However, it isn't always a librarian that he finds to participate. For example, in March 2012, Michael attended the Massachusetts Library Association conference and met author Andrew Blum, who was promoting his latest book *Tubes: A Journey to the Center of the Internet*. While the topic of this book isn't specifically library related, Michael thought that the author would be an interesting person to interview, and in July 2012, Blum was our guest for Tech Talk.

The other difference between the Tech Talk episodes and the others is that Michael generally shares a bit of technology news and tips at the end. In preparation for this, Michael again keeps his eye on social media, looking for news on security issues, new technologies, tools, and tips that might be of interest to the viewers.

Promotion

The library commission hosts listservs for librarians in the state. From the beginning, NCompass Live was announced on the state librarian listserv and on the commission's NCompass Blog. Each Friday, Christa sends a reminder message to the listserv about the next week's show. When the archived recoding is ready, an announcement is also sent. Periodic reminders about NCompass Live are posted to the blog but not every week.

Christa also sends messages out via the commission's Twitter feeds. There is a general news feed[6] and a tech-specific one.[7] At the same time that the messages are sent to the listserv, Christa sends the same message to the commission's Twitter news feed. Depending on the topic of an NCompass Live, a message is also send to the tech feed. The hashtag for the show is #NCompLive.

To further promote the show, Christa created a Facebook page for NCompass Live in 2012.[8] Show updates are now posted there first; then, she switches to administering the library commission's own Facebook page and shares the NCompass Live posts there.

Production

On the day of the show, Christa sets up the webcam and laptop in our meeting room. On the meeting room computer, she logs into the GoToWebinar session for that show. Then she logs into the show on the laptop, where she can monitor the session's broadcast quality and audience questions. The library commission uses Yawcam,[9] free webcam software, to run our webcam. The camera window is resized to a small size, next to the presentation or webpage view, so that both will be shared via GoToWebinar. A rotating set of PowerPoint slides are shown, giving attendees instructions on how to use GoToWebinar.

If the speakers are in the meeting room with her, Christa gives them brief instructions on how they will be using GoToWebinar. If the speakers are attending remotely, she will check in with them to make sure they have successfully connected. When we are ready to start the show, Christa will switch to showing the speaker's presentation, or she will hand over control of GoToWebinar to the remote speaker. When she is ready to go live, she starts recording in GoToWebinar and introduces that week's show (Figure 2.1).

During the show, the audience is able to ask questions either via text chat or with a microphone. Christa uses the laptop to track questions and pass them on to the speakers to respond to.

When the show is over, Christa stops the recording and closes the GoToWebinar software. The software then begins converting the recording from the proprietary GoToWebinar format to a WMV format. Depending on how much video and live webpage sharing there has been during the show, this conversion could take anywhere from minutes to hours.

Postproduction

After the GoToWebinar file has finished converting, Christa does a quick check to make sure it was successful. Sometimes there is a glitch in the conversion, and she has to use the Microsoft Expression Encoder software to manually convert it. This can take another 1 to 2 hours. Once she has a good WMV file, Christa uploads it to the commission's YouTube account.[10]

If the speaker had slides or other documents as part of their presentation, Christa uploads them to the commission's SlideShare account.[11] She also saves any websites that were mentioned during the session to the commission's Delicious account.[12] In Delicious, all NCompass Live links are tagged

Figure 2.1.   Broadcasting NCompass Live.

with *ncompasslive* and a phrase unique to that episode so that they can easily be linked to as a group.

Finally, Christa creates the archived episode entry in the library commission's training calendar. This is a copy of the original entry for the live show. Christa adds links to the YouTube recording, the SlideShare files (if any), and the Delicious links for that episode. This entry is added to the Archived Sessions page for NCompass Live.[13]

When the recording entry is ready in the training calendar, Christa announces its availability on the commission mailing lists, Twitter feeds, and the NCompass Live and library commission Facebook pages.

Once Christa has published the archived copy of the episode on the commission's website, Michael then takes over and converts the episode into an audio-only recording for the commission's NCompass Podcast.[14] Podcast episodes are mostly generated from NCompass Live shows but can also include content from other events, such as live presentations given by commission staff or others at events sponsored by the commission. In either case, if we have a video of the event, the process of converting it into a podcast episode is pretty much the same.

The first thing that Michael needs to do is to create a separate audio file from the video. Here he runs a conversion from the WMV video file to a WAV audio file using VLC.[15] Next, since in many cases the audio from the presenter is louder than, say, the audio from an audience member asking a question, he runs the WAV file through Levelator.[16] All Levelator does is create a copy of the WAV file with the audio levels much more even than in the original.

The next stage is to import the WAV file into Audacity,[17] where most of the actual audio editing and postproduction are done. First Michael opens a previously recorded file that contains the opening and closing music, along with a voice track that goes along with the closing music, inviting listeners to the next episode. Early on in the podcast, Michael would customize this piece to include the subject of the next episode. However, with continued schedule changes, this proved to be inaccurate more often than we liked, so a standard closing voice-over was created.

Next Michael imports the leveled WAV file into the Audacity project and gives that track a once-over, looking for extended pauses from technical difficulties during a recording. This does not happen very often. Next he will trim the track at the beginning and end to remove extra silence and any other extraneous audio from the beginning and end of the episode. Then he will align the audio from the episode to start at the end of the opening music track and end prior to the closing music track.

The next stage involves recording a customized voice-over for the opening music track. Here he will open a Word document containing the script for the opening voice-over. He will update the episode number, insert a new brief description of the episode, and change the text regarding the length of the episode and when it was recorded. Once that is all up-to-date, he will read it out loud a few times, put on his headset mic, and record the text directly into the Audacity project at the correct location. Often, he is able to record this in one or two takes, but he has also been known to need nearly a dozen takes once or twice.

Once all the audio is recorded and aligned in the project, it is saved and archived as an Audacity project just in case the master files are needed in the future (Figure 2.2). The final step for the audio is to export it to a 128-kb MP3 file with the appropriate metadata and to copy the resulting file onto the web server.

Once the MP3 file is on the commission's web server, the RSS file for the podcast needs to be updated, and the new episode needs to be announced on the commission's blog. To update the RSS feed, Michael uses ListGarden.[18] This small program runs in a web browser and uses a form-based interface to create and edit RSS code. In this case, Michael runs the program and chooses

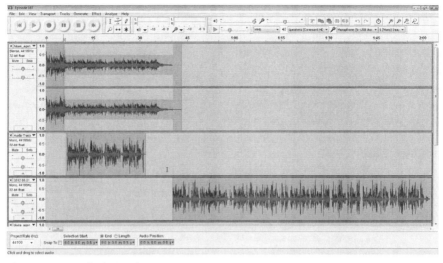

Figure 2.2. Audacity project.

to add an item to the podcast feed. He then fills in such information as the episode title, description, and URL of the MP3 file to be attached. When finished, ListGarden generates the needed code and saves the updated RSS file to the web server. To make sure it all worked as it should, Michael then launches iTunes and updates his subscription to the podcast. If nothing went wrong, the new episode and related metadata promptly download for him. If he finds anything wrong at this point, it's back to whatever stage in which the error occurred for an update.

To create the blog post for the new episode, Michael logs into the NLC WordPress installation, copies the content of a previous podcast post, and uses that as a basis for a new post. He updates the title, description, and links accordingly and publishes the post.

Typically, the publication of the video recording and the podcast of an episode happens within 24 hours of the original broadcast. However, due to Christa and Michael's travel schedule, sometimes it can take a bit longer.

WHERE WE ARE NOW

As of mid-August 2012, there have been 177 episodes of NCompass Live, with 3,210 live attendees. Due to staffing changes at the library commission, our statistics for archived sessions are incomplete. But based on our historical data, the number of views of our recordings is at least double the live attendance. Some of our most popular topics have been anything cataloging related, marketing, Google+, grant funding, and the annual Summer Reading Program updates by our children's and young adult coordinator, Sally Snyder.

Over the 3.5-year life of the show, we have missed broadcasting the show only a few of times, for technical issues. We broadcast every week of the year, except the week of our state library conference.

NCompass Live is based in Nebraska, and the reason for starting our show was to provide information to Nebraska librarians. However, the topics of many of our episodes are broad enough to be useful to librarians located anywhere. NCompass Live is free and open to anyone to watch—the cost and production is the same for an audience of 10 or 100. So we welcome anyone who wishes to watch our live show or our archived recordings. As a result, the show has now developed a national audience.

NCompass Live has been a great success for the Nebraska Library Commission. The response from library staff across the state has been overwhelmingly positive. Christa regularly receives suggestions for show topics from both inside and outside the commission. And the expanded national audience has, of course, benefited the commission with more exposure and interest in its programs and services.

We are often asked, "How do you do this every week?!" The only answer is "We just do." Having the support of the library commission administration has definitely made producing NCompass Live easier. We strongly believe that having this buy-in, support, and encouragement has greatly contributed to the increased success of the show, and with this support, we plan to continue making NCompass Live an important resource for librarians across Nebraska and beyond.

The authors have provided related screenshots and photos of the equipment and websites involved in this project on Flickr@http://www.flickr.com/photos/librarycommission/sets/72157632117786692/.

NOTES

1. http://nlc.nebraska.gov/NCompassLive/.
2. http://www.amazon.com/Megapixel-Webcam-Camera-Laptop-Noteboo/dp/B001M53FX6/ref=sr_1_1?s=pc&ie=UTF8&qid=1345400270&sr=1-1&key words=webcam.
3. http://www.usa.canon.com/app/html/HDV/XHA1S/.
4. http://www.bluemic.com/snowball/.
5. http://www.gotomeeting.com/fec/webinar.
6. https://twitter.com/nlc_news.
7. https://twitter.com/nlc_tech.

8. http://www.facebook.com/NCompassLive.

9. http://www.yawcam.com.

10. http://www.youtube.com/user/nebraskaccess.

11. http://www.slideshare.net/nebraskaccess.

12. http://delicious.com/NLC_Reference/.

13. http://nlc.nebraska.gov/NCompassLive/NCArchivelist.asp.

14. http://nlc.nebraska.gov/Feeds/NLCPodcast.xml or https://itunes.apple.com/us/podcast/ncompass-podcast-audio-video/id576497533.

15. http://www.videolan.org/vlc/index.html.

16. http://www.conversationsnetwork.org/levelator.

17. http://audacity.sourceforge.net.

18. http://www.softwaregarden.com/products/listgarden/.

3

Digital Reference That Supports E-Learning at the University of California

TEAL SMITH AND DONALD BARCLAY
University of California, Merced

HISTORY AND BACKGROUND

Library digital reference services, in the broadest definition of the term, first surfaced in the mid-1980s as librarians and library users began conducting reference transactions via e-mail. In the more narrow sense of real-time chat-based digital reference, the origin date is some time during the final year or two of the 20th century. In November 2001, by which time some 200 U.S. libraries were using chat-based reference, the University of California (UC) Libraries Task Force on Digital Reference released "Expanding Reference Services for the University of California: A White Paper on the Relevance of Digital Reference Service to the UC Libraries." This document surveyed the current state of digital reference in academic libraries as well as the technology issues surrounding digital reference services. The authors considered the many challenges, opportunities, and policy issues that were emerging alongside digital reference services, and they concluded by surveying the current use of digital reference; across the UC, four campuses—UC Los Angeles, UC Irvine, UC Berkeley, and UC Davis—were testing or using commercial software to provide real-time digital reference services, while UC San Diego was investigating digital reference software. Staff at all five active campuses reported some frustration with the digital reference software they were using, and the authors of the white paper concluded that the lack of a clear front-runner among the various software packages was hindering implementation of digital reference service in the complex and diverse UC system. The white paper concluded with recommendations pointing to a single shared digital reference service as the ultimate solution for the UC system. If anything was clear from the early forays into digital reference, it was that no campus library had enough staff resources to provide more than token service on its own.

In June 2002, the UC libraries formed the Digital Reference Common Interest Group (Dig Ref CIG), charging it with assessing the staffing issues surrounding digital reference and producing a list of criteria for digital reference software packages; tellingly, the charge stopped short of calling for the implementation of a systemwide digital reference service. During the course of 2003, the Dig Ref CIG issued three reports: one addressing the desirable features of digital reference software, a second addressing staffing issues, and a third evaluating five of the leading digital reference software packages available at the time.

In the spring of 2004, members of the UC libraries Dig Ref CIG began seriously discussing the piloting of a UC systemwide digital reference service, proposing in October 2004 the five goals for the pilot:

- provide excellent service,
- add a new service point,
- extend reference hours,
- show the value of a collaborative reference service, and
- determine the usefulness of chat reference to the participating libraries.

The campus with the most hands-on digital reference experience, UC Irvine, provided the initial training for the other UC campuses participating in the pilot: Los Angeles, Merced, Riverside, Santa Barbara, and San Diego. A Dig Ref CIG subgroup created guidelines and assembled campus policy manuals to help digital reference staff answer frequently asked questions about campuses other than their own. The California Digital Library picked up the initial cost of the shared 24/7 digital reference software package and established a listserv so that digital reference staffers could ask questions of one another and generally share experiences and expertise. The UC libraries launched the digital reference pilot on January 9, 2005, with the intention of running it through March 25, 2005; in the end, the pilot was extended through June 9, 2005. Operating from 6 P.M. to 9 P.M., Sunday through Thursday, the digital reference pilot was open for 165 hours during winter quarter 2005 (January 9–March 25), fielding during that time 334 UC digital reference sessions. As anticipated, the number of sessions peaked during the busy middle of the quarter and tailed off as the quarter ended. The average length per session was 10 minutes, while the median was 7.

At the end of the pilot, a survey asked those who volunteered to staff the digital reference to respond to the statement "In general, the quality of service patron's received has been excellent." Twenty percent responded *strongly agree*, while 80% responded *somewhat agree*.

During the course of the pilot, a total of 32 users of the digital reference service (9% response rate) chose to complete a pop-up survey asking questions about their just-completed digital reference experience. Twenty-six (81%) users who responded rated the service quality as "All the information I needed"; 5 (16%) rated it "Helpful, but not complete"; and one (3%) rated it "Not helpful at all." Eleven users (34%) indicated that getting an answer quickly was the best feature of the service. When asked what they liked least, 22 (69%) respondents either left the field blank or reported that they experienced no problems with the service.

After reviewing the pilot, the Dig Ref CIG recommended that the UC libraries

- adopt digital reference as a permanent service beginning in fall 2005,
- provide support so that all 10 campuses could participate,
- allow any nonparticipating campuses to join at any time, and
- apportion the cost for the 24/7 software among the participating campuses.

The initial success of the UC digital reference service convinced UC library leadership to continue providing the service beyond the June 2005 ending date. Though the service officially remained a pilot, it was, in reality, operating as a production service. By April 30, 2007, the UC digital reference service had fielded 2,360 questions from students and faculty at 8 of the 10 UC campuses. In a report written by UC Dig Ref CIG cochairs Elaine Adams and Ken Furuta, the authors identified the following obstacles to moving from pilot to an official production service:

- a lack of fully developed policies and procedures, including training guidelines, service standards, best practices, and regular transcript review procedures;
- effective promotion and marketing;
- better up-front presentation of end-user instructions for accessing licensed electronic information resources;
- longer service hours and, as a result, greater staffing commitments from the participating campuses; and
- the appointment of a systemwide digital reference service coordinator.

In October 2008, the UC libraries began placing on their webpages the qwidget—a software application that, much like an IM (instant messaging)

box, makes access to digital reference service more seamless for end users. In January 2009, the UC campuses joined the QuestionPoint Academic
Reference Cooperative on a trial basis through June 2010. The UC libraries
contracted to provide 40 hours of QuestionPoint Cooperative service per
week while opting to commit an additional 10 hours per week to staffing the
UC-only queue. For the first time, users of the UC digital reference service
had around-the-clock access to a librarian, a fact reflected in a surge in use:
There were 19,000 UC sessions from the start of around-the-clock service
in January 2009 through June 30, 2009. The volume was so great that most
campuses were double staffing to meet the demand for service. In spite of this
success, by the end of 2009, half the UC campuses still relied on volunteers to
staff their service hours, and only 4 of the 10 campuses were staffing evening
hours. That by 2009 the UC campuses, like most higher education institutions
across the country, were experiencing severe budget cutbacks made the staffing shortages all the more difficult to overcome.

A major technical difficulty arose when the UC joined the QuestionPoint
Cooperative. The popular qwidget interface directed patrons into a queue that
only UC librarians could see, rather than "rolling up" into the QuestionPoint
Cooperative queue. This meant that UC campuses had to devise less-than-
ideal workarounds to meet the needs of UC users who accessed the service at
times when UC librarians were not on duty.

On June 30, 2010, some 5.5 years after the initial UC systemwide experiment, digital reference finally went from being a pilot to being an official
production service. Besides discovering that digital reference is a service that
attracts a great deal of use, what did the UC libraries learn as they moved
from pilot to production?

MOST OF OUR FEARS WERE GROUNDLESS

As the UC libraries grew more familiar with digital reference, it soon became
apparent that most of the things we worried about in theory turned out to be
nonissues in practice. For example, as the digital reference service was being proposed, some were concerned that nobody would use it or that those
who did would be unhappy with the quality; neither of these proved to be
true. There was also fear that the service would be overwhelmed by hordes
on non-UC-affiliated users, but that scenario never transpired. Privacy, both
for librarians and for users, was a concern, but the digital reference software
has proven to be as secure as anything on the Internet can be, and there have
been no reports of breaches or unauthorized snooping into other people's
business. In practice, digital reference staff routinely forward questions to
a user's home library for further assistance knowing full well that the tran-

script containing everything that the user and the staffer typed will be read by someone else. Yet another early concern was whether or not nonsubject specialists could answer highly subject-specific questions and how such questions might be routed to qualified subject specialists. As it turns out, most digital reference questions do not require subject specialists, and when they do, digital reference software allows questions to be referred to the patron's home library for further assistance.

Along similar lines, there was a strong initial feeling that cobrowsing, in which the digital reference provider and the digital reference user share a web interface, would be a crucial feature of any digital reference software package. It did not take long, however, to realize that cobrowsing was technologically impractical and unnecessary. Concerns about whether digital reference could be as instructional as in-person reference largely fell to the wayside, as it became apparent that staff who wished to do so could work instruction into their responses when it seemed appropriate.

TRAINING AND POLICY

Effective training and clear policies proved to be essential to successfully implementing digital reference service—at the time, an unfamiliar and slightly weird concept for most librarians. The most obvious training need was preparing staff to use digital reference technology. This need was met through a combination of instruction, documentation, hands-on practice, mentoring, and periodic refreshers. The second and less obvious training need was preparing staff to operate in a chat-based environment where such familiar cues as tone of voice, body language, and eye contact are totally missing and in which the timing is more like that of a continuous exchange of short e-mail than a real-time in-person or telephone encounter. In the chat environment, it is quite possible (if not exactly relaxing) for a skilled digital reference staffer to handle three simultaneous sessions with none of the patrons being the wiser, a feat that seems impossible to someone who has never staffed chat reference.

Besides providing the right kind of training, it is important to have policies that clearly define what is expected of a digital reference staffer. For example, the UC policy states that no staffer need take more than one patron at a time, though working with multiple patrons is not forbidden. Other elements of policy define how to handle a rude or pranking patron, what rules dictate passing a patron to another digital reference staffer, and when to refer patrons to their home library for further assistance. To be effective, policies need to be documented and made available to digital reference staffers. Adherence to policy is further enhanced by providing digital reference staffers with prewritten scripts they can use to do politely welcome a patron, end a session, or warn a patron that their behavior is inappropriate.

ADMINISTRATIVE SUPPORT

If anything took the implementers of UC's digital reference service by surprise, it was how popular the service became in such a short time. While this success was welcome, it put a strain on a system that did not employ enough staff to meet demand. When the members of the UC Dig Ref CIG approached library leadership for additional staff resources, they and their leaders (who were largely supportive of digital reference) ran up against some harsh realities. Higher education was at the time entering a period of reduced funding from the state and federal government, so the simple option of hiring new staff was not available; worse, most UC libraries were reducing staff through attrition and even contemplating the prospect of layoffs. The alternative of assigning existing staff to digital reference, though possible, was complicated by a number of factors. Moving staff to digital reference would leave staffing gaps in other necessary services. Some staff did not want to do digital reference, and forcing them to do so could turn into a human resources nightmare of rewritten job descriptions, formal grievances, violations of existing collective bargaining agreements, and general workplace unhappiness. Rather than having a full-time digital reference service coordinator to oversee training, scheduling, and assessment of digital reference service for the UC libraries, these tasks fell to the members of the Dig Ref CIG, who could dedicate only a small part of their time to those tasks.

Of course, it is not as if the UC library leadership has done nothing to support digital reference. Each campus has regularly come through with its share of the QuestionPoint Cooperative annual membership costs, and in 2012 the UC libraries approved an increased payment that would, at last, solve the qwidget rollover problem. On at least some campuses, participation in digital reference has evolved from voluntary to mandatory, and in some cases, job descriptions for new positions are now including digital reference among the list of required duties. More administrative support for staffing the service would, however, ease the chore of providing digital reference service and allow for more improvements in the quality of the service.

ASSESSING THE SERVICE AS IT GROWS

Much of the ongoing assessment of the UC digital reference service is informal and performed at the campus level. The QuestionPoint service includes a survey option, so day-to-day feedback is received through patron surveys completed immediately following a chat. Some campuses also review patron transcripts on a regular or semiregular basis. This allows the reviewer to follow up with the patron as needed. QuestionPoint chats can be referred to a librarian at the patron's home institution when the chatting librarian feels that local follow-up would be beneficial; however, as with any shared service, perception of service can vary, and a librarian reviewing transcripts later may stumble upon a question that needs follow-up but wasn't formally marked for it by the chatting librarian.

An overview of usage is completed each month when the designated UC Dig Ref CIG librarian pulls together monthly statistics on the service. The statistics provide a broad snapshot of total and per-campus usage volume and are added to a larger yearly document, allowing for an easy review of the year to date (Table 3.1). Included in the monthly statistics are measures of accepted chats per campus, number of questions accepted by a UC librarian (as opposed to a cooperative librarian), chats requested by day and by time of day, and number of chats coming in through the UC libraries' shared catalog.

Other assessments have tended to follow a transcript analysis model. UC Irvine, UC Merced, and the California Digital Library have all completed local or targeted transcript analysis projects; a small systemwide analysis has also been completed. Although time-consuming, transcript analysis can provide useful insight into multiple areas of interest.

One area of interest is quality of service. This has been investigated informally as part of a broader transcript analysis focus by simply noting issues or patterns of issues in how librarians are assisting patrons. Poor service quality can be due to a variety of causes, most of which can be easily addressed. For example, librarian customer service skills may be improved by creating or updating training for staffers; some difficulties that external librarians have when assisting the local library's patrons may be improved by clarifying information—or making it easily findable—on the library website. A more formal service quality assessment would benefit from using a rubric like the Maricopa Community Colleges' Ask a Librarian Rubric (developed by Karen Biglin and the MCCCD Ask a Librarian Committee), available at http://libguides.maricopa.edu/AskaLibrarian_Rubric.

Most transcript analyses at the UC have focused on gaining a better awareness of (1) how patrons use the digital reference service and (2) what types of questions they most commonly ask. This focus gives libraries the opportunity to improve communication efforts: The questions asked by patrons can support changes to webpages, initiate the creation of specific library guides, and so on. Digital reference transcripts can also inform decisions or policies in the works; for example, a review of noise complaints received via digital reference assisted UC Merced librarians in deciding whether to maintain, expand,

Table 3.1.   University of California Digital Reference Statistics, 2011–2012 Academic Year

Time	Count
12–1 am	406
1–2 am	231
2–3 am	134
3–4 am	105
4–5 am	68
5–6 am	73
6–7 am	109
7–8 am	224
8–9 am	494
9–10 am	924
10–11 am	1,405
11–12 pm	2,061
12–1 pm	1,960
1–2 pm	2,002
2–3 pm	2,083
3–4 pm	2,075
4–5 pm	1,831
5–6 pm	1,488
6–7 pm	1,227
7–8 pm	1,121
8–9 pm	1,123
9–10 pm	926
10–11 pm	792
11–12 am	514

Table 3.2. Top 10 Most Frequently Asked Questions

Topic		No. of Questions
1	Finding specific articles	28
2	Research help—choosing databases	22
3	Virtual private network and off-campus access	19
4	Finding and using databases (including e-book databases)	14
5	Finding specific books and e-books	13
6	Finding scholarly articles	12
7	Research help—choosing keywords	11
8	Finding stats	10
9	Help citing, using RefWorks	9
10	How to request items from other libraries (interlibrary loan)	5

Note: Based on digital reference transcript analysis at the University of California, Merced—November 1, 2010.

or get rid of a designated quiet study floor in the library. In addition to addressing specific assessment goals, this analysis focus simply provides an interesting snapshot of student information and research needs (see Table 3.2).

Transcript analysis can also be used to investigate a specific issue—for example, the analysis done by the California Digital Library to review questions that came into the chat service from the new UC systemwide library catalog (see Figures 3.1 and 3.2). The transcript analysis supplemented other assessments in highlighting what patrons were experiencing with the new catalog.

NEXT STEPS

As the UC shared digital reference service has grown and matured, the campuses have brainstormed and investigated options for further improving the service. Some improvements have been desired for a long time, while others are newer goals. One aim is to branch out and expand our staffing models. Some campuses have a greater challenge in finding staffers because of local models that make staffing the digital reference service voluntary rather than mandatory for reference librarians, and for all campuses, it continues to be difficult to find librarians to staff the service in the evenings. Some staffing ideas that have been discussed are utilizing library and information science interns and hiring part-time staff or librarians who would be solely responsible for digital reference service.

Another idea that has been discussed is to create a position or role for one individual to serve as central administrator of the service. This proposal was suggested as far back as 2007 in the report authored by UC Dif Ref CIG cochairs Elaine Adams and Ken Furuta. The Dig Ref CIG still oversees the UC digital reference and is led by two cochairs, who serve for 2-year terms. Often, the cochair who has served longer handles administrative duties, such as systemwide scheduling and communication with QuestionPoint contacts, for 1 year before retiring as cochair. Although there has been minimal turnover in the group, having one individual responsible for administrative work over the longer term would create greater consistency in that area for everyone involved.

Regardless of whether UC digital reference is able to secure a central administrator, greater consistency will also be improved by more thorough succession planning. With one Dig Ref CIG cochair position retiring each year and with entirely new leadership occurring every 2 years, creating and maintaining documentation that details scheduling and other administrative processes as well as decisions the group has made (including "when" and "why") is critical. As the service has become more established, the Dig Ref CIG has begun to think more about succession planning. One recent accomplishment in this area was the discussion about and the creation of shared service expectations. Once completed, these were added to the UC digital reference wiki for use in training and for general reference by all UC digital reference staffers.

UC is also exploring the possibility of setting up separate QuestionPoint queues for some campuses. This would create a queue where only one campus's patrons would enter, although these questions would eventually roll into the cooperative queue if not picked up. For a staffer, it can certainly be more challenging to assist patrons at another campus or institution; with a separate queue, staffers who are uncomfortable working with external patrons can staff the campus queue only. For larger campuses with hundreds of digital reference questions per month, monitoring the campus queue during heavy traffic times would cull questions from the larger pool while making use of librarians who would otherwise be unwilling to staff the service.

TIPS WHEN TAKING THE LEAP

Plan for succession. Keep track of decisions that are made, including when the decision was made, who made it, and why. With any project or service that lasts an extended period, there is a good chance that old decisions will be rehashed without being realized. Keep detailed documentation for the administrative and logistical areas of the service, and make sure that it is easily accessible for all who need to access it. Documentation created for UC digital reference varies from a highly detailed calendar of tasks for scheduling to outlined procedures on reviewing transcripts to a simple to-do list when there is turnover in the systemwide group.

Have mandatory staffing when possible. Staffing digital reference is less challenging for coordinators when it is required of some librarians rather than entirely voluntary. The staffing scheme should be flexible enough to capitalize on individuals' skills while still ensuring that there are enough librarians to maintain stable staffing of the service. Work digital reference into job descriptions when possible, especially for new hires.

Create and maintain initial and ongoing training for staffers. Not all librarians are comfortable with the technology and mode of delivery; some may be unsuited for staffing the service, while others are simply uneasy about trying something different. Creating a structured training plan will help ease staffers into the task. The initial training for new staffers can include basic information about what the service is and why the library is doing it. If the service has been in place for a while, training can include examples of questions that have been asked in the past. Ongoing training sessions are also important. These can give staffers the opportunity to ask questions or voice concerns and learn about new features or upcoming changes to the service. The Maricopa Community Colleges' Ask a Librarian Rubric can come in handy during training sessions: Select two or three digital reference transcripts that highlight problems or positive service quality, and ask staffers to review them and then grade the transactions using the rubric. The rubric activity can be especially effective when done in pairs or small groups and then discussed as a larger group. Including patron quotes about the service or other indications of service popularity in the training may help boost staffers' interest and pride in the service. Of course, continuing open communication via the usual internal channels is just as important as holding formal training sessions.

Take advantage of digital reference transcripts to improve the service itself or other areas of the library. This can be done as part of a formal transcript analysis project or simply by reviewing transcripts more informally on a regular or occasional basis. Reviewing transcripts provides an opportunity to discover and address problems with the digital reference service—for example, problems with the technology or a staffer's lackluster customer service skills. Transcripts can also assist with improvements to other areas of the library by shedding light on where patrons have difficulty with the library website, policies, or space. These sample patron experiences can highlight where things are working or not working in the library, informing small fixes or supporting larger changes.

Promote and place wisely. As with any service or positive change being rolled out to the community, promotion is key. Some marketing tactics employed at the UC to advertise digital reference have included promotion e-mail, posters and table tents, digital signage, and marketing videos. An equally important promotional strategy is simply the placement of digital

Figure 3.1. University of California, Santa Barbara, library poster, April 2009.

Figure 3.2. University of California, Berkeley, library poster, April 2009.

reference chat links on the library website and associated pages. Placing chat links on top-level pages of the library website as well as within the catalog and library research guides will boost usage. Just be aware that heavier promotion will lead to more traffic, so be prepared with appropriate staffing levels or an easy way for patrons to send their question via e-mail or another channel just in case the service is busy or unavailable.

The UC digital reference service has continued to be highly successful. While the usage growth has, for the most part, tapered off and is showing signs of stabilizing, overall usage remains high. In the 2011–2012 academic year, UC patrons initiated over 23,000 sessions. For some campuses, the number of requests ranged from 12% to 14% of fall enrollment. Comments such as "Wildly helpful as always!" and "Such a lifesaver!" from the optional closing survey continue to highlight the popularity of the service.

4

The Critical Thinking Skills Initiative: An Information Literacy E-Learning Collaboration

BARBARA CARREL, JANE DEVINE, ANN MATSUUCHI, AND STEVEN OVADIA
City University of New York Libraries

The Critical Thinking Skills Initiative (CTSI) was developed by the Office of Library Services of the City University of New York (CUNY) and funded by a Verizon Foundation Grant. It was a pilot program to create e-learning opportunities to teach information literacy, digital fluency, and critical thinking skills to community college students. Focusing on these skills, the initiative had the ultimate aim of supporting the university's efforts to improve academic achievement, increase student retention and graduation rates, and equip community college students with the skills necessary to successfully compete in today's digital marketplace. A netbook was distributed to each student enrolled in the pilot as an incentive to register and complete the CTSI courses. The netbook also provided a means to level the technological playing field and facilitate the online coursework and, ultimately, student success. To evaluate student learning and, thereby, the efficacy of the CTSI courses, the project utilized a pre- and postcourse iSkills assessment exam from the Educational Testing Service, a leader in educational research and assessment. LaGuardia Community College, a CUNY school, played an important role in the CTSI, from the development of the grant proposal to teaching the courses for the pilot and participating in the assessment phase.

INITIAL EFFORTS

The primary component of the CTSI—to provide associate degree students with competence in information literacy as a means of increasing critical thinking skills—was intended as a key intervention in hopes of improving academic success. Not only are many community college students across the nation academically underprepared, but their educational institutions are experiencing high attrition rates. According to a *New York Times* article on CUNY's New Community College, the national statistics show that "only about one in five students graduates within three years. Most never do, and never transfer to a four-year college" (Perez-Pena, 2012, p. 18). The CUNY Office of Library Services believes that information competence—finding, evaluating, and communicating information from a range of technology sources and applying it for specific purposes—is critical to these students' academic and professional careers.

A committee of CUNY administrators and teaching and library faculty from the Office of Library Services, the School of Professional Studies, and three CUNY community colleges (LaGuardia, Kingsborough, and Hostos) participated in the program. Administrative endorsement was secured and registration pathways strengthened across and between the participating community colleges to support student enrollment and ensure credit trans-ferability. Given the imminent fall 2011 semester launch date, the Office of Library Services decided to utilize two established CUNY online infor-mation literacy courses rather than create a new one: two sections of the one-credit Internet Research Strategies (LRC 103) course, developed by librarians at LaGuardia Community College, and one section of the three-credit Digital Information in the Contemporary World (COM 110) course, taught in the CUNY School of Professional Studies online BA program. Each online course brought its own perspective—one mostly application based and the other theory based—focused on teaching students how to acquire the skills necessary to find and evaluate information and apply it to specific research problems. With the use of netbooks, students would also improve their digital fluency and their ability to communicate effectively in an electronic environment.

Individual marketing materials were produced for each CTSI online class and disseminated on all three participating community college campuses to-ward the end of the spring and the beginning of the summer 2011 semesters. Promotional flyers highlighted the free netbook opportunity, provided course descriptions, outlined course perquisites, and announced the point person designated on each campus to facilitate the atypical registration process for these classes. The goal was to register 60 students to allow for dropouts while ensuring a total cohort of 50 students needed to receive the Educational Testing Service's institutional data reports. Although only 59 students from LaGuardia, Kingsborough, and Hostos community colleges registered for the two courses, the minimum cohort for the Educational Testing Service's pur-poses was attained. Of the 59 students who registered, 46 students completed LaGuardia's LRC 103 course (of those 46, only 2 were from campuses other than LaGuardia Community College) and 6 completed the School of Professional Studies online BA's COM 110 course (all students from either Hostos or Kingsborough community college).

After evaluating a number of netbooks, the CTSI planning committee selected the Hewlett-Packard Mini 1103 netbook, loaded with Windows 7 Starter and Microsoft Office Starter. The planning committee also established program criteria whereby students would qualify to have ownership of the netbooks transferred to them at the semester's end. Ownership required a passing grade of C– or higher for coursework and mandatory participation in both the pre- and postcourse iSkills assessment. Netbook contracts delineated the specifics of these conditions and were to be signed by each enrolled student at the time of the precourse iSkills assessment and netbook distribution. Netbooks were loaned to students using the library's regular circulation system for the duration of the semester. In the end, all students completed the course and met the program's criteria, and outright ownership was transferred to each student at the completion of the fall 2011 semester.

The Educational Testing Service's iSkills assessment is a proctored outcomes-based tool that presents "real world," scenario-based tasks. Two cohorts were created through the service's online iSkills assessment administrative site for the initiative—a pre- and postcourse cohort to ascertain the impact of the CTSI courses on students' information literacy skills. Five customized questions were added to the precourse assessment to reveal students' English-language skills and their previous experience with library instruction. Questions were also added to the postcourse assessment to gauge students' incentive for registering and their overall perceptions upon course completion. Assessment administration was coordinated across all three community college campuses with a variety of dates and times provided to accommodate CUNY's diverse student population.

LAGUARDIA COMMUNITY COLLEGE'S PARTICIPATION

LaGuardia Community College is located in Long Island City, Queens, New York. College enrollment includes over 16,000 matriculating students and many more nonmatriculating in adult and continuing education programs. The diversity of the student body matches that found in New York City, with over 128 languages spoken on campus. Students study in 50 major and certificate programs in areas in the allied health fields, business, technology, and liberal arts studies. LaGuardia's student's graduation rate is near 25% within 5 years, close to the national norm.

The LaGuardia Community College Library wanted to participate in the CTSI for several reasons. The initiative presented an opportunity to showcase the library's online Internet Research Strategies course (LRC 103), with the potential of attracting students from other campuses. LRC 103, developed in 2005, has been popular with students in both its face-to-face and online iterations. The nature and content of the course seemed to lend itself for consideration for the CTSI program, and, indeed, its syllabus and assignments had been reviewed in the process of the creation of the grant proposal. The class is a liberal arts elective, and the library markets it each year to students who are eligible to take the course.

The CTSI project also offered the opportunity to have LRC 103 assessed via the iSkills test in a pre- and postapplication. The course is regularly assessed in two ways mandated by the college. Students rate instructor performance using the Student Instructional Report form, an electronic version of which is used for online courses. The other means of assessment is a peer observation. For the online course, the practice has been for the peer observer to review all the materials used during a 1-week period, including instruction materials, group discussions, homework assignments, and all public student contact with the professors. Then the observer meets with the faculty member (or members) to discuss the reviewed materials and make any suggestions that might help improve performance, documenting his or her comments for the faculty member's record. This principally means giving feedback about the instructor's effectiveness. With the iSkills assessment, there would be additional information about course outcomes and students learning.

Participation offered other benefits as well. LaGuardia's students would gain from the opportunity to take the course and would receive a netbook for their efforts, an attractive incentive. The CTSI also fostered collaboration with other CUNY campuses and the Office of Library Services. And there was the promise that if the CTSI could win additional funding for a second year, there would be the opportunity to develop a three-credit online course that LaGuardia could add to its program offerings. The LaGuardia library, as the only CUNY community college library that offered for-credit courses, felt that it should take a lead in this initiative.

The chief librarian contacted the CUNY Office of Library Services when she first heard that the grant proposal was under development. The library's experience with teaching information literacy online was a good resource for the project. Discussions involved the library's teaching faculty who provided course syllabi, course outlines, and teaching assignments. The final grant proposal included the names of LaGuardia's chief librarian, Jane Devine, and Louise Fluk, the coordinator for the library's instruction program.

IMPLEMENTATION

Implementing the CTSI at LaGuardia required agreement about several issues. LaGuardia agreed to teach two special sessions of LRC 103 for CTSI during the fall 2011 semester. To be eligible for the course, a student would have to have already accumulated 15 credits and meet the regular prerequisites of the course, to have completed one of several basic skills writing courses. Advertising materials were sent by e-mail and snail mail to all students identified as being eligible to take the course. Interested students were asked to come to the library to discuss the course with a project librarian. This procedure was followed so that students could be advised of the nature of the course and its technology requirements. This conversation also explained the required participation in the iSkills pre- and postcourse assessment and the need to achieve a C– grade or better for the course to keep the netbook offered as incentive. Many students responded, and within a short time, library staff began to keep a waiting list. All the students were registered at one time by special arrangement with the registrar's office. If a student dropped out during the registration period, staff contacted the next person on the waiting list. By the end of the registration period, the classes were full, and some students had to be turned away.

The library called on two of its most experienced professors to teach the CTSI sections, Steven Ovadia and Ann Matsuuchi. It was decided early on that the course would not be adapted in any way for the purposes of the CTSI, especially with regard to helping students prepare for the iSkills assessment. While there was a temptation to "teach to the test," it was agreed that the class would stand as it was currently being taught so that the assessment would give a clear picture of the effectiveness of the course.

While the courses were delivered online, students did have to come into the library twice for the pre- and post-iSkills testing. The students had the option of several days/times when they could come to take their tests. At the pretest, netbooks were issued to the students after they had signed the form stating their obligations under the initiative. Students were also instructed on how to use their new netbooks and how to seek technical support if needed.

TEACHING THE ONLINE COURSES AT LAGUARDIA

As a one-credit course, the LaGuardia library's LRC 103 translates to an hour of instruction per week during a 12-week semester. CTSI required two sections of the class, but since the instructors decided to use the same online platform, they decided to team-teach the two classes, in effect creating one "super class." Each instructor graded the work of the students in one's official section, but both interacted with students outside their sections, whether face-to-face, via e-mail, or within the discussion forums. Interestingly, a number of students did not seem to pick up on who their official instructor was and interacted primarily with their unofficial instructor. Coteaching, or team-teaching, can prove advantageous for instructors and students (Scribner-MacLean & Miller, 2011). While both instructors had taught LRC 103 as a fully online class, the two had not taught the class together. At LaGuardia, the fully online version of LRC 103 is frequently taught by two librarians, with an instructor experienced in teaching online paired with one who has little or no online teaching experience. Having two experienced instructors allowed for the rapid evolution of ideas, regarding both content and delivery. It made it easier to develop assignments and to evaluate them.

In terms of workload, a fully online class represents more work than one might expect. While the instructors were freed up from having to lead a class at a specific time and place each week, the asynchronous nature of a fully online class can sometimes feel like a class that will not end. Since instructors do not normally get face-to-face time with each student, commenting on posts and submitted work becomes especially important as the only chance for students to get feedback on their work. Teaching online requires more involved commenting than what the instructors might have to give in a face-to-face class. The workload issue was not unique to the CTSI classes, but the CTSI students proved to be more engaged than their counterparts in other online sections of the course, which tend to experience more attrition over the course of a semester. That so many students were so actively engaged in the class did produce more work to the instructors.

These learning objectives are met by expanding students' understanding of how the digital landscape currently operates and how the delivery of various kinds of information has changed in recent years. The class content emphasizes evaluation, with students encouraged to deconstruct sources to determine if they are appropriate and reliable for a given research need. The online nature of the CTSI class, which required students to communicate electronically with their professors and with one another, also helped to impart students with a digital fluency.

The goals of the LRC 103 class appear in the class syllabus:

> Students can expect to be taught the following concepts and skills necessary for both academic and professional research:
> 1. an understanding of the history of the Internet and gain familiarity with digital communications
> 2. how to choose appropriate Web-based information sources and use them successfully

3. how to formulate and modify search strategies in order to retrieve needed resources successfully
4. critical evaluation of electronic information resources

Class content was not limited to the instruction of mechanical skills; it went beyond giving students experience using different kinds of search tools. The theme of the class was dynamic, focusing on issues relating to Internet research, from the politics that govern information access to the confusing state of online content creation. In addition to Google Books versus electronic books, the class covered the history of search engines, library subscription databases versus Google Scholar, the fundamentals of source evaluation, blogs and the future of journalism, Wikipedia, the census as a research tool, and copyright and intellectual property.

With the intent of enabling multiple modes of learning, the structure of each week's class usually included readings or videos, with assignments to be completed independently, as well as forum discussions that involved students in both sections of the course. The forum posts were usually more conceptual, with students sharing their perspectives on the week's topic, as informed by the readings or videos from that week or previous weeks. For instance, one lesson examined how Google Books compares to library-subscribed electronic books, and students were asked to consider if Google Books could function as a business or a library.

CREATING A LEARNING SPACE WITH THE RIGHT PLATFORM

Choosing the right classroom platform is key to stimulating the right level of class engagement, especially in an e-learning situation. "Look and feel" as well as usability are crucial aspects to consider to maintain student interest. While LaGuardia offered the Blackboard learning management system, prior experiences with Blackboard's less-than-ideal usability led the instructors to decide on an alternative for the main classroom space. The class was "held" in a Ning-created site, but the midterm and final were administered using Blackboard, which has a robust test manager. Ning (http://www.ning .com) is a customizable social networking platform, with free basic-featured accounts provided for educational users. Unlike popular social networks such as Facebook, which are open to all users, Ning can be configured as a closed network, meaning that registration could be limited to CTSI students. The instructors invited students into the class, and each student created a Ning profile, which included some basic prompts that the instructors designated: what the student wanted to be called, his or her major, any languages spoken, and the gendered pronoun preference.

Control over self-presentation in online classrooms provides a beneficial alternative to traditional spaces, allowing for a leveling of otherwise estranging differences. For example, a transgendered student could invisibly use a chosen name without being questioned at its variance from the one on record. Students could also upload a profile picture. All of this was optional. Many students felt comfortable enough to customize their profile areas with photos and information that helped create a sense of community, but a few left everything blank.

The dynamic appearance of the Ning class site as well as its accessibility via mobile devices motivated a greater level of responsiveness from both students and instructors. Class content was posted in forums, which allowed students to begin commenting on content immediately and right below their work for the week. Ning places a profile picture next to every response, letting students not only read what their classmates were posting but also see, in a virtual manner, the classmates themselves (for those who chose to post profile photos). Ning also supports threaded commenting, which allows students to respond to individual posts rather than simply present one post after another. So if Student A posted something early in a thread, Student B could respond to that post later, with the subsequent post immediately below the earlier one, linking the two by proximity. The string of comments could also be viewed immediately on a page without having to click on individual subject lines, as is standard in older discussion board formats, such as the one used in Blackboard.

The class's seventh assignment, "Blogs and the Future of Journalism," represented a typical week for the class. The first part required students to do some brief readings about the roles of blogs in journalism and to watch a video about blogs by journalist Scott Rosenberg. While the content was ostensibly about the role of blogs in journalism, it reinforced the idea of the importance of evaluation and the notion that the expertise of the author is what determines whether a source is reliable. After finishing the readings and videos, students were asked to discuss the trustworthiness of blogs in a post of at least 50 words. For the second part of that week's work, students were asked to write a long paragraph explaining how they decide to trust a blog for personal or academic use. Through the public work posted in the Ning forums and the private work sent to the instructors via e-mail, the instructors were able to gauge the evaluation skills of the students and orient them toward what is significant to consider. These criteria would apply for all content, not just for blogs, and the evaluation process would be repeated in assignments throughout the semester so that, slowly, students learned how to determine if a work was reliable, without becoming distracted by the format of the work.

The online format has the potential to allow for equal access, a more level playing field, which can be a challenge to maintain in face-to-face classrooms. The coursework becomes largely self-paced, outside of general weekly deadlines, allowing students to make needed adjustments or request additional assistance. Communication tools, such as real-time chat windows for contacting instructors when available, were utilized in a number of instances. Content can be more easily customized for students with particular needs. Captioning on videos and textual scripts can be provided so that non-native English speakers and students with disabilities have multiple options for absorbing the material.

THE CTSI STUDENTS

The CTSI students were atypical for a number of reasons. Students had to register in person with the library's coordinator of instruction, unlike most students, who are usually able to self-register online using the college's registration system. One of the biggest challenges in conducting a fully online class is starting up the weekly routine for students to "check in" on the classroom site. The in-person registration helped with class start-up by allowing the instructors to collect preferred working e-mail addresses for students. Usually, early communication with students is conducted through student college e-mail accounts, which, unfortunately, many students do not check regularly. There is, therefore, often a lag at the start of the semester, as some students are confused about how and when the class meets. Having working, monitored e-mail addresses early in the semester enabled the instructors to get students on the same page earlier than usual.

Students can also be less likely to respond to messages from instructors whom they have met only virtually. The iSkills precourse assessment provided an opportunity for the instructors to meet their students briefly, with one or both instructors introducing themselves and giving a short overview of the expectations of the class. A working relationship among students and between the students and the instructors resulted from these scheduled in-person testing sessions. To a limited extent, these structural differences made these classes resemble the hybrid teaching format, which combines both face-to-face and online instructional methods. Research on online learning has pointed out how nomenclature is inconsistently used—that is, "online learning" can refer to a range of tools and pedagogical approaches (Bowen, Chingos, Lack, & Nygren, 2012, p. 7).

The netbook incentive also promoted—indeed, ensured—commitment to performance in the class. To keep the netbook after the semester concluded, students were required to earn at least a grade of C–. This condition made them conscientious about turning in work, which is not always the experience with non-CTSI students. The level of student-to-student interaction and the quality of the work submitted also seemed greater than in non-CTSI sections. Overall grades were based on a number of factors: online midterm and final exams (25% of the final grade each), individual written components (40% of the final grade), and participation in group forums (10% of their final grade). Around 81% of the student cohort reported that the netbooks they received enabled better class performance. In their pursuit of maintaining a C–, most students considerably overshot, with just four students earning the bare minimum grade required to keep the netbook. The effect of the netbook is also evident in the comparison of fall 2011 CTSI students with spring 2012 non-CTSI students, whose class, like the fall 2011 class, was fully online and taught by the same instructors. Of the 46 fall 2011 students, 69% got at least an A–, compared to 38% in the spring 2012 class, which had 39 students. Around 22% of fall 2011 students got a B–, B, or B+, compared to 23% in spring 2012. Just 8% of fall 2011 students got either C or C–, compared to 20% of spring 2012 students. And no fall 2011 CTSI students got lower than a C–, while 6% of spring 2012 non-CTSI students did. Also, 13% of spring 2012 students got a WU grade, which is given to students who stop showing up to a class without officially withdrawing. The fall 2011 classes had no official withdrawals.

While one might assume that students were taking an online class to avoid coming to campus, a few students came by the library regularly to connect with their LRC 103 instructor. Online learning should not be conflated with distance learning, particularly in the context of commuter student populations. A number of students reported a preference for the convenience of an online class—not so much to avoid face-to-face contact with a professor and to avoid ever coming to campus but rather to reduce the need to be on campus at a specific time. Anecdotally, it seemed that many students worked while on campus but appreciated the asynchronous flexibility that a fully online class provided.

The CSTI students resembled conventional online LRC 103 students in a few ways. The majority of students had never taken online classes before, and some expressed anxiety about unfamiliar procedures. In-person registration and iSkills assessment sessions allowed for management of some of these concerns.

The role of the iSkills test was a source of confusion, given that scores on this test had no bearing on the actual course grade. Although the screeners and instructors emphasized that LRC 103 grades would not be based on iSkills performance, many students wanted their iSkills pretest grade, believing that it would be factored into their final grade for the class. In addition, some students almost missed the final exam for the course because they were under the impression that the iSkills postcourse assessment was the final exam, despite the instructors' explanation that the iSkills test was conducted to test the effectiveness of the course itself, rather than individual performance.

PROJECT OUTCOMES

The Educational Testing Service bestowed its valued iSkills Critical Thinking Skills Certificate on those students who received a score of 260 or more (out of a total of 500 possible points) on either the pre- or postcourse assessment. A total of 20 CTSI students (38% of the total cohort) received an iSkills certificate "for having demonstrated applied critical thinking and problem solving skills in technology-enabled education and work scenarios." The certificate—which was signed by Kurt Landgraf, president and CEO of the Educational Testing Service—may prove to be extremely valuable in the future employment pursuits of these students. According to the *Wall Street Journal*, employers have long complained that many college graduates lack precisely the skills recognized by this certificate: critical thinking and problem solving (Taylor, 2010, p. 2). An electronic version of this certificate was e-mailed to each student to be used as a "digital merit badge," or an electronic display of valuable job-related skills. Anne Eisenberg (2011) recently reported a trend among job seekers electronically displaying such certificates and awards demonstrating specific job-related merits (p. 3).

Of the 52 students who completed the CTSI classes, the posttest scores of only 6 remained the same as the pretest (11.5% of total cohort); 37 student scores increased from 10 to 160 points, with an average of 55 points higher on the postcourse assessment (71% of total cohort); 16 students increased their score by more than 50 points; and 5 students increased their score 100 points or more. Only 9 CTSI student scores decreased in the posttest, the range being 10 to 80 points, with an average of 33 points lower on the postcourse assessment. Of those who received an iSkills certificate, scores increased from 0 to 160 points, with a 62-point mean increase.

The program's netbook incentive proved to be a significant draw for registration, a major motive for personal commitment and effort, and the main cause of ultimate success. This conclusion was validated by the customized additional questions in the postcourse iSkills assessment. Eighty-six percent of the student cohort registered for the course because of the promise of full ownership of the free netbook at the end of the course; 81% admitted that the potential of keeping their netbooks increased their class participation, commitment, and, ultimately, their success. Moreover, an overwhelming majority of students, 92% (all 48 students who responded to the question), reported that they would recommend the class to a fellow student.

The LaGuardia library achieved some of its goals in participating in the initiative. It did get assessment feedback about LRC 103 showing that students benefited from taking the course. LaGuardia students did get the opportunity to take the course and walk away with a netbook and, in some cases, a certificate of proficiency in critical thinking.

Even as the CTSI sections were being taught during the fall 2011 semester, however, CUNY was beginning to reconsider general education requirements across the university. This evaluation has involved all the community colleges in reviewing their courses and programs and reconsidering elective courses, such as the library's information literacy courses. The CTSI's long-term objectives of developing a new three-credit online course and further opportunities for e-learning collaborations had to be abandoned, as did the plans to track the performance of participating students as they enter the job market. There remains the hope that all that was learned through the CTSI can contribute to a future project.

REFERENCES

Bowen, W. G., Chingos, M. M., Lack, K. A., & Nygren, T. I. (2012). Interactive learning online at public universities: Evidence from randomized trials. *Ithaka S+R*. Retrieved from http://www.sr.ithaka.org/research-publications/interactive-learning-online-public-universities-evidence-randomized-trials

Eisenberg, A. (2011, November 19). For job hunters, digital merit badges. *New York Times*, p. 3.

Perez-Pena, R. (2012, July 22). The new community college try. *New York Times* (Education Life suppl.), p. 18.

Scribner-MacLean, M., & Miller, H. (2011). Strategies for success for online co-teaching. *Journal of Online Learning and Teaching, 7.* Retrieved from http://jolt.merlot.org/vol7no3/scribner-maclean_0911.htm

Taylor, M. (2010, September 12). Schools, businesses focus on critical thinking. *Wall Street Journal*, p. 2.

5

Cutting to the Quick: Library Instruction in the Age of Happy Distraction

Lura Sanborn

St. Paul's School Library

Slightly over a year ago, after searching YouTube for product reviews, I became absorbed by cosmetic tutorials. I continue to watch and seek them out, my appetite, curiously, never waning. I check my subscription box daily and become excited when one of my favorite beauty gurus has a new post available to watch.

My adoration is powerful, and I began to wonder if I could successfully apply some of the appealing features of these beauty tutorials to my library instruction classes, with the intention of making library instruction more attractive to my students. So, in addition to appeasing my vanity and desperation to disguise ever-creeping aging, I began analyzing the engaging nature of these tutorials, trying to figure out the magic spell and then apply it to my library classes.

In truth, everybody is busy, and everybody has something they'd rather be doing (anyone else catch the jennasmarble video on app addiction? [*Apps Are Ruining My Life*, 2012]). Even so, YouTube beauty tutorials are something I will find time for, and certain gurus, such as Pixiwoo (2012), Wayne Goss (2012), and Lisa E (Eldridge, 2012a), consistently capture my attention, from beginning to end. After watching even more YouTube (*research!*) and discovering Lilith Moon (Lilithedarkmoon, 2012) and Tina Georgy (2012), I believe there are some key elements that can be taken from beauty tutorials and applied to library instruction.

FINDINGS

Time

Most videos run about 10 minutes in length. Many gurus mention in their videos their intention of keeping things short, even sometimes apologizing when they feel as though a video is getting too long. Videos are occasionally longer when devoted to answering questions and when a particularly complicated, many-step look is being taught.

Focused Content

Tutorials typically focus on one specific look, one specific technique, or one specific product. Tutorials are never a cosmetology program in one video.

Likability

My gut tells me this is the most important finding: The folks are likable. My favorite gurus are clearly experts; in fact, five of my six favorites are professional makeup artists, some with seriously impressive dossiers (Callen, 2012). Yet, they don't come off as dogmatic or offensively didactic. They come off as kind, approachable, friendly—sort of like a next-door neighbor that's stopped by for a chat. Lisa E provides a great example (Eldridge, 2012b); judging by the comments, this is a viewer favorite, too.

Impressive teachers, indeed. As people and teachers, they are surprisingly authentic, and therein, I believe, lies a large piece of the likability quotient.

Accessible Information

This casual-feeling approach makes the information easier to absorb somehow. To further help, not only are products and application techniques talked through in the video tutorial, but products are listed in the downbar beneath the video and often posted on a guru's accompanying blog. There is no burrowing about or time lost floundering, searching for the right product.

APPLICATION

I began reworking my lectures and programs in the fall of 2011 and continued the model through the academic year. Typically, I am provided a copy of a given research assignment a week or so in advance. (Really, it depends on the faculty member, as I will be contacted anywhere from a day or a month in advance.) I then, unsurprisingly enough, build a research guide prior to meeting the class.

The following are the elements that I tried to emulate in my reworked library instruction classes. Like most of us, I eagerly read articles based on the ERIAL study (DePaul University, Illinois Wesleyan University, Northeastern Illinois University, University of Illinois at Chicago, & University of Illinois at Springfield, 2010), which appeared in 2011. While remodeling my classes, I kept both the attractiveness of YouTube tutorials and the available ERIAL information in mind.

Time

My aim was to keep informational and demonstrative lectures to 20 minutes or less, budgeting 30 minutes of class time to accommodate for questions and comments.

Focused Content

This naturally stems from cutting lecture time to 20 minutes. I remind myself that I am not running a master of library science program and that, in fact, this is not graduate school–level research. I tend to focus on two or three highly relevant skills or sources most helpful to completing the assignment and let the more complete LibGuide be the comprehensive source. This pairs nicely with the reflection in the *Higher Ed* piece summarizing the ERIAL study: that librarians and professors tend to project an idealized version of research while, in fact, only a very small percentage of the students whom we are working with will become career academics performing and meeting true academic research requirements (Kolowich, 2011).

I work from the LibGuide during class and reinforce that it is a comprehensive and always-available resource (along with the friendly librarian). As an example, I visited all junior-level humanities classes during their annual capstone research project. For those classes visited within the first week of the assignment being distributed, the presentation focused on how to find a topic, one eReference collection, and one major eBook collection. The remaining classes I visited the following week, and these students had already turned in three potential topics. In this case, I focused on eReference, one major eBook collection, and one digital eNewspaper archive. My intention was to present information to complete the immediate task at hand (finding a topic, getting background information on that topic) as well as then presenting sources to aid in successfully completing the next step (eBooks) or two (eNewspapers). Of course, there's more to research than these steps, and not all projects will require or be satisfied with these exact sources; this is where the LibGuide and its extensive information are mentioned and enforced as well as my promise to respond to follow-up questions outside of class.

Accessible Information

Accessible information is perhaps the easiest component, as the LibGuide provides the perfect display case for those resources most helpful for a given assignment. Databases and research sources are presented cleanly within the LibGuide interface and make a great launching point for in-person lectures as well as a referral point for students throughout the research process. As gurus mention "dupes," or additional products in the downbar or associated blog, the LibGuide is the place to put additional and comprehensive sources not mentioned during the library class. The LibGuide also shows off the bigger picture. For beauty gurus, the bigger picture is ultimately them: their career, their product line, their recognition and following. In a recent SAGE/LISU study (LISU, Loughborough University, & SAGE, 2012), one librarian suggested that the library is doing too good of a job: that patrons don't realize that the digital resources selected and paid for by the library are not in fact widely available and completely free. This, I think, is part of the bigger picture for libraries. At the start of class, I always mention that the sources that will be discussed are provided and paid for by the school—that these resources live behind a paywall, and for students at the institution, access is paid for by the school. This same information is stated on the top page of the corresponding assignment LibGuide. Since doing this over the past year, I've noticed that students do demonstrate a small response upon hearing that the resources are paid for by the school. I'm inclined to think that the resources take on more value to patrons when it is clear that the resources cost money.

The likability quotient is, of course, the hardest one; there's no clear formula to achieve this. I do my best to not take things too seriously, to be well informed, to speak honestly about the products used, and to smile and make lots of eye contact. I've heard that liking one's field can also help. It happens that I'm naturally rather enthusiastic about research; "enthusiasm is contagious," I've been told (fingers crossed). I do try to take this one with a pinch of salt. The amount of hate that YouTubers receive is notorious. YouTubers receive a magnitude of hateful comments, and some gurus have devoted entire videos to addressing this stressful and hurtful situation. Isn't it Abraham Lincoln who is frequently misquoted as saying, "You can please some of the people all of the time and all of the people some of the time but you can't please all of the people all of the time?" Being reasonable, informative, and kind, I feel, is a good starting place.

I try to mimic the comments section in YouTube by mentioning my availability to answer questions outside of class, via e-mail, or in person. It also seems to me that part of the appeal of YouTube is that it comes to people, when people want it: on demand. While I can't be 100% on demand, I can at least go to a given class, in a regular classroom. This keeps students in their comfort zone and eliminates the inevitable loss of class time, having kids trudge over to the library building or having everyone lose time while waiting for the student or two who forgot that class was in the library today.

AIMS AND OBJECTIVES

For me, the aim of library instruction is always to let students (and faculty) know that there is a friendly, approachable person in the library (who loves research), that is there to help them with any element of their research, whether that means locating sources, participating in one-on-one tutorials on specific research products, or receiving citation assistance. The secondary goal is to impart a little knowledge in direct conjunction with the assignment—that is, how to locate a topic, understanding the difference between primary and secondary sources, why do we care what the difference is between the library's digital reference collection and Wikipedia? The aim of this program was to complete the first and secondary goals but by consuming less class time.

NEXT STEPS

The majority of my institution's academic classes are held in two buildings: one for languages and humanities (humanities being the department with the most research projects and the one that requests 90% of the library instruction classes) and one for science and math. I have often wondered about the efficacy of myself, as the research and instruction librarian, being housed on another part of campus, away in the library. I've joked about having a satellite office in the building housing our humanities classes. It seems to me that I should be where the students are, particularly where they are working on research and where research assignments are being distributed. Having regular office hours in this classroom building would allow for "drive-by" reference: answering questions and helping students with research during their free periods and during passing time between classes. I would like to be more available to faculty too, especially during class time. I would like faculty to be able to ask me into their classroom in the moment when a question about eBooks, locating a topic, or journal searching comes up.

FRESHMAN PROGRAM

A planned direct application of this short, direct minilecture style is a new proposed freshman digital literacy program. To begin, I spoke with the chair of our freshman humanities teaching team. I proposed the following: If he could share the yearlong curriculum with me, I could study this over the summer. During this time, I would identify points in the curriculum where a simple, in-person, YouTube-style library lecture could easily be inserted. The skill and the topic would support and mesh with existing curriculum. Any resultant student-produced product, designed to test the skill, would be assigned and evaluated by the freshman faculty, although I will be happy to assist in assignment design and assessment. The aim would be one library session with each section of freshman humanities per trimester, with room for growth in upcoming years if the pilot program goes well.

My proposal was received positively. So far, it's still summer, and I'm reviewing the curriculum. Come fall, I will meet again with the freshman humanities chair to run through my summer brainstorming.

Clearly, an additional important next step is to create friendly, informative videos delivered by an individual, much like the ever-popular beauty tutorials. Seeing a product and its application, as done by a human, helps make the processes clearer and more obvious. I'll have to screw up my courage this year, get over my self-consciousness, and begin banging these out. My plan is to create short videos, each focused on a particular research source or theme or step, and in 10 minutes or less explain the what and the how of it. These can then be embedded within the appropriate LibGuide. Currently, I'm thinking that these may launch as a pairing to the aforementioned freshman program, with a LibGuide containing these embedded video tutorials, which builds throughout the year in conjunction with the program.

Another project is to create videos that represent or pair with each box in the research flowcharts (Figure 5.1). I created the flowcharts in the spring of 2011, really on a whim. They felt a bit self-indulgent to build. Yet, I've received great feedback on these from faculty and students alike. During one library instruction session, the corresponding faculty member, upon seeing the flowchart in the LibGuide, said that she was going to print one out for each member of her class. The following year, a junior caught me in the cafeteria to say that she was told I was visiting her class soon for an instruction session and to ask, was there a flowchart for the junior research project this year like there was last year for the sophomore project? This helped me understand the value of visual communication. It is my hope that instructional videos will be helpful in this same vein.

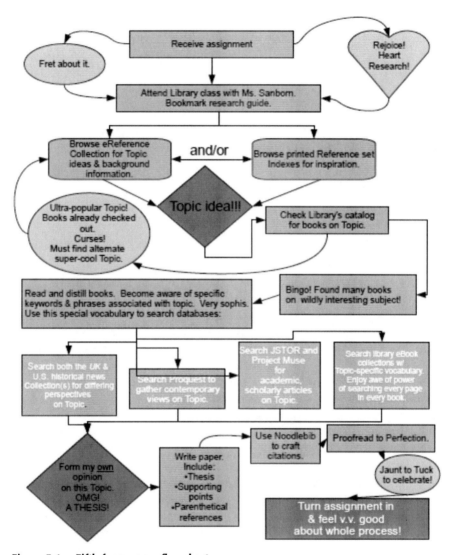

Figure 5.1.   Fifth form paper flowchart.

My thinking is that videos will support existing library instruction and research guides. The videos would serve as review and reinforcement and, ideally, as another demonstration that somebody friendly and interested is available via the library to offer research support.

The videos would also live on the library's YouTube channel. I began building this experimental channel a year ago. So far, I have focused on creating tutorials with no face, just voice-over. JingPro (soon disappearing and being replaced with Snag-It) was used to created tutorials explaining the library's eBook collections, eBook collection features, Noodlebib citations, Noodlebib note cards, and a step-by-step guide to using the catalog and library map and then plucking a book from the shelves. Xtranormal was also used to create animated tutorials explaining eReference and the eResource Finder. Xtranormal is now behind a paywall, even for educators, and I therefore expect no more will be created by me. These little videos were a good tiptoe into creating video tutorials, and they got me thinking about visual presentation and communication. Hopefully, this experience will be helpful when thinking about more person-presented videos.

RESOURCES (STAFF, FUNDS, TIME) REQUIRED

This project was a reformulation of current lectures and presentations. Time was required to recraft the lectures, and as more classes were requested this year than last and even though the lectures were shorter, the reworking, travel time, and additional classes did take up more time than last year.

In terms of product and technology needed in moving into the next phase— namely, shooting video containing a librarian—a camera will be clearly be needed. The library owns a fancy camera (Canon EOS Kiss X5), and our IT department has several to lend, if I want to try different models. Guru Michelle Phan uses iMovie (Humphrey, 2011) to edit her million-view tutorials; surely then, this software will be good enough for me! My library recently purchased a staff MacBook with iMovie loaded on it.

Time is also needed to research tools and train on them to create videos. I've been using JingPro to film computer screen–based video; this is currently $19.95 a year, although the product is being discontinued and will be replaced by SnagIt, which is $39.95 a year. Minor video editing was done in YouTube, which is free.

In terms of staffing, at my institution, research and instruction is staffed by one, so this was done with one librarian (*c'est moi!*). My library is lucky to have an excellent in-house tech gig. It's been extremely productive to talk through some of the tech elements and bounce ideas and current questions/ theories with this helpful individual. I happen to be a big fan of embracing the temporary: What works well today may need to be reconceptualized to work well tomorrow. While certain technology may be spot-on for a current project, I think it worth looking forward and finding that which works better as things evolve. My institution is small enough to experiment, and if our hands to get a little bloodied, it's easy enough to step back.

ASSESSMENT

Embarrassingly enough, I have done no formal assessment of the service. I do have a bit of anecdotal evidence: Faculty who have requested one library instruction class have invited me back for a second session and, in some cases, into classes I had not previously visited. Shockingly, some classes have ended with spontaneous student applause. While repeat customers and clapping students are appealing, certainly I do need to investigate and employ a more accurate and official means of information literacy assessment, built on something such as the SAILS or TRAILS model or at least a carefully crafted online survey.

Speaking of anecdotal, the humanities department does carry out a student survey/assessment of the research paper assignment, after the paper has been turned in. This year, some faculty were kind enough to share with me that several students had indentified the library instruction session as helpful and, in some cases, the most helpful part of the research process.

ANY ADVICE?

I hesitate to mention this, almost fearing that it may suddenly occur at my institution. For all the good that would come with it, at my school faculty status comes with a whole host of time-eating responsibilities: endless meetings, committee work, advising students (and their parents!), dorm duty, dance chaperoning, sport coaching. Having said that, if an institution is serious about information literacy, those that are teaching and developing this same information literacy curriculum would be that much more effective when provided faculty status. This accomplishes a few advantages to the institution, including taking some onus off the librarian to continually justify or prove the value of their work as being as important as other skills taught in the classroom. Obviously, for an individual employee representing oneself and a larger department, it is always important to demonstrate good work and value, but the institutional support makes it clearly understood that the campus values said digital literacy curriculum, and it is more than a hobby being peddled around by a librarian. (Unless, of course, a librarian is lucky enough to be teaching one's own stand-alone digital literacy class! Now there's some institutional support. Otherwise, we are dependent on others inviting us in.)

The ERIAL study determined that students regard librarians a "glorified ushers"; indeed, when asked if librarians were regarded as research specialists, "one senior psychology major told the researchers, 'I don't see them that way. I see them more like, "Where's the bathroom?"'" (Kolowich, 2011).

Who's going to seek out research help from a bathroom usher? At my institution student perception regarding faculty status, education, and perceived value is quite keen. Faculty status implies that it is understood that a degree of higher education has been achieved, thus, in the student mind, changing the perceived value of librarian work.

While it's okay to be humbly knowledgeable, fun, and friendly in fact, I would say these qualities are rather essential to a successful program), teaching is still time-heavy and valuable work. Institutional support is critical; a librarian is not an island: We must be healthily integrated into the larger academic ecosystem. Future thoughts: Perhaps as libraries become ever digital and as physical spaces become less important (for both classrooms and libraries), teaching librarians will travel more, answer more questions received digitally, and become evermore embedded (Hall, 2008), thus helping that integration become more easily adopted and accomplished.

CONCLUSIONS

I would venture that YouTube is home to those that will one day be considered our time's artists and philosophers. Perhaps today's blogs will too be looked at in the way we now look at the latest Dickens serial installment arriving by boat, across the Atlantic, almost 200 years ago.

Pair with that the ever digitally growing library content, which seems to simultaneously ensure that the library grows increasingly complex to navigate. Access is easier; quality materials are abundant; and patrons are more confident than ever in using digital and technological tools. Yet, the abundance of resources can make pinpointing the right source and understanding the difference between the myriad of sources complicated, especially for young researchers.

Twenty years ago (my high school years, gasp!), there was a card catalog for locating books and the *Reader's Guide to Periodical Literature* for locating magazines (most of which my little library didn't own). Now, libraries routinely offer such widely varied products as the Gale Digital Archives, hundreds of thousands of eBooks contained in different platforms, JSTOR, ARTSTOR, digital reference collections from different providers, magazine archives from EBSCO and ProQuest, archival newspapers from Accessible Archives, and stand-alone archived periodical titles from Gale, such as *National Geographic*, or *Vogue* from ProQuest. Hundreds of different digital products exist from dozens and dozens of providers/interfaces. And these are just selections from a potential library subscription lineup, never mind the freely available treasures from sources such as the Haithi Trust, LOC, and the

Internet Archive. And then there's all that confusing junk and Internet trash out there. Understanding just the research process can be difficult enough, let alone navigating a library webpage and trying to understand and then select which resources would be most helpful.

Sometimes it is such blessed relief to not read information. While it seems likely that some tenants of good librarianship will remain timeless (accessibility, responding helpfully and meaningfully, with accuracy), as we move deeper into the 21st century, utilizing techniques and styling both used by and appealing to patrons seems only appropriate and relevant. Instructional videos and in-person lectures based on the casual yet informative YouTube style mesh with our ever increasingly visual society. The visual medium is powerful, and when it's presented as friendly and fun, the appeal factor is unignorable. And appealing gets more attention.

REFERENCES

Apps are ruining my life [Video file posted by JennaMarbles]. (2012, July 11). Retrieved from http://www.youtube.com/?v=bRKOB2xY4Ao&list=UU9gFih9rw0z NCK3ZtoKQQyA&index=2&feature=plcp

Callen, Karena. (2012). *Lisa Eldridge: About.* Retrieved from http://www.lisaeldridge.com

Eldridge, L. (2012a). *Lisa Eldridge make up artist* [YouTube channel]. Retrieved from http://www.youtube.com

Eldridge, L. (2012b, July 17). *Meeting the EX—Chat/up therapy* [Video file]. Retrieved from http://www.youtube.com/?v=HKY4O0RIn0M&feature=player_embedded#!

DePaul University, Illinois Wesleyan University, Northeastern Illinois University, University of Illinois at Chicago, & University of Illinois at Springfield. (2010). *Ethnographic research in Illinois academic libraries.* Retrieved from http://www.erialproject.org

Georgy, T. (2012). *Tina Georgy beauty* [YouTube channel]. Retrieved from http://www.youtube.com

Goss, W. (2012). *Gossmakeupartist* [YouTube channel]. Retrieved from http://www.youtube.com

Hall, Russell A. (2008). The "embedded" librarian in a freshman speech class: Information literacy instruction in action. *College and Research Libraries News, 69*(1), 28–30.

Humphrey, Michael. (2011, September 21). Michelle Phan: On beauty, Bob Ross and future success. *Forbes.* Retrieved from http://www.forbes.com/sites/michaelhumphrey/2011/09/21/michelle-phan-on-beauty-bob-ross-and-future-success/

Kolowich, Steve. (2011, August 22). What students don't know. *Inside Higher Ed.* Retrieved from http://www.insidehighered.com/news/2011/08/22/erial_study_

of_student_research_habits_at_illinois_university_libraries_reveals_alarmingly_
poor_information_literacy_and_skills

Lilithedarkmoon. (2012). *lilithedarkmoon* [YouTube channel]. Retrieved from http://
www.youtube.com

LISU, Loughborough University, & SAGE. (2012, July 16). The final report [blog].
Working Together: Evolving Value of Academic Libraries. Retrieved from http://
libraryvalue.wordpress.com

Pixiwoo. (2012). *Pixiwoo* [YouTube channel]. Retrieved from http://www.youtube.
com

6

Developing and Sharing an Open Source Software Tool That Supports Online Interactive Learning

LESLIE SULT

The University of Arizona Libraries

Many academic libraries across the country, if not the world, are facing the same stark reality—student enrollment is on the rise while budgets and the ranks of qualified staff are cut to the bone. To cope with this situation and to ensure that students continue to receive necessary instructional support, libraries increasingly look to online instruction to fill the gap created by the reduction in library personnel and resources. While various strategies and related software are currently available for developing online instruction, many librarians encounter significant barriers—technical as well as time and cost limitations—that prevent them from successfully adapting or utilizing these tools. This chapter discusses the creation and release of an open source tool that, once installed, allows librarians to quickly and easily create online interactive tutorials that are both engaging and pedagogically sound. Because this tool is open source, libraries are free to tailor it to meet their individual needs or continue to collaborate with other institutions to augment and improve its functionality for what is becoming a growing community of dedicated users.

HISTORY

The University of Arizona Libraries (UAL) has long experimented with methods for providing innovative and scalable instruction to the university's 39,000 undergraduate, graduate, and professional students. Over the years, UAL librarians have developed a variety of methods to support these students, including webpages, screencasts, and flash-based interactive tutorials. While all are useful in certain circumstances, each has its drawbacks. Webpages tend to lack interactivity, while screencasting and flash editing

63

software can be expensive and frequently involve steep and time-consuming learning curves. UAL librarians therefore wished to find a less expensive and more user-friendly alternative or develop one of their own.

THE FIRST ITERATION OF THE SIDE-BY-SIDE TUTORIAL: HELP FOR THE ABSENT STUDENT

Because the majority of general education classes offered at the University of Arizona are quite large, it was not uncommon for a significant number of undergraduates to miss the librarian-led, one-shot library instructional sessions scheduled by their instructors. During the fall semester of 2000, UAL reference librarians began collaborating with programming staff to address this problem by creating an online alternative that was still hands-on and authentic. With the goal of providing an active learning experience, the librarians and programmers created a web-based tutorial to guide students through a series of research steps. The tutorial's design allowed students to follow directions and fill in answers on one side of the page while manipulating a live webpage on the other side (hence, the "side-by-side" nature of the tutorial). When completed, students e-mailed their responses to a librarian as well as the course instructor. The librarian reviewed each submission and provided individualized feedback regarding the student's topics, keywords, search strings, and so on. The tutorial was offered in 2001 as a pilot program, and initial student assessment and reviews were very favorable. Indeed, it quickly became apparent that the online, side-by-side tutorial format was an effective means of providing meaningful library instruction to a large number of students (Figure 6.1).

Given its initial success, UAL librarians began investigating whether use of the tutorial could be expanded to reach more students. By 2002, the side-by-side tutorial format was incorporated into a number of courses, including those offered by the university's English composition program, which enrolls approximately 5,000 students a year. While well liked by students and instructors, the initial iteration proved to be time intensive for librarians and programmers. The reason for this was twofold.

First, the tutorials were constructed in such a manner that a substantial amount of librarian intervention was required after the content was developed and delivered. In particular, the creators of the original side-by-side tutorial sought to replicate an in-class session as closely as possible. However, unlike a traditional library instruction class, during which a librarian presents an exemplar topic and then assists students with their own topics as needed, the creators decided to allow students to work through the tutorials using a

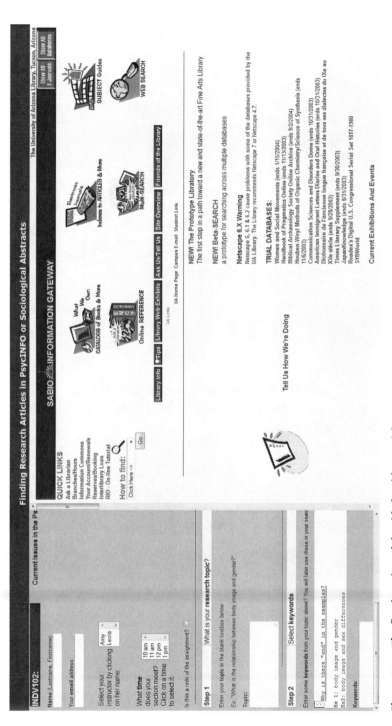

Figure 6.1. The first iteration of the side-by-side tutorials.

topic of their own choosing. This open-ended approach required librarians to provide individual feedback to each student who completed a tutorial, irrespective of whether it was necessary or desired. Had librarians opted not to provide individualized feedback, students would have been left not knowing for certain if they had successfully completed the assigned tutorial. Given the large number of students who were using the tutorial, the sheer volume of tutorials submitted for review and comment quickly became overwhelming.

The second factor was that creating and editing each tutorial involved a multistep process. Specifically, the librarian responsible for a tutorial's content had to first save it as a Word document. The Word document was then forwarded to the programmer, who used it to develop the tutorial. The librarian and the programmer would then communicate with each other to make any necessary modifications. When it came time to revise an existing tutorial, the librarian usually started by copying the existing web content into a new Word document since it was often the case that the original Word document, if it could be found, did not reflect changes made after it was initially sent to the programmer. The result was a great deal of communication between the librarians and programming staff as well as a large and unwieldy number of documents being shared back and forth, both of which frequently lead to miscommunication and errors.

THE SECOND ITERATION: SHARING THE BENEFITS (AND THE BURDENS)

By the 2005–2006 academic year, a number of significant changes to the side-by-side had been implemented (Figure 6.2). From a technical perspective, the tutorials received a major graphic overhaul and were modified to allow printing. Logistically, a new approach to the tutorials was adopted that would help relieve some of the crushing workload for librarians, who had found themselves unable to keep up with the demands of responding to the large volume of tutorials.

Although the tutorials still relied on a model requiring individual feedback, the responsibility for providing the feedback was shifted to the course instructors, at least insofar as the English composition program was concerned. Before making this change, however, the UAL invested significant time and energy to train instructors in the English composition program on high-level information literacy concepts as well as on how to teach students to perform effective database and library catalog searches. After they were trained, the English composition instructors began using the tutorial as a preassessment for in-class research instruction.

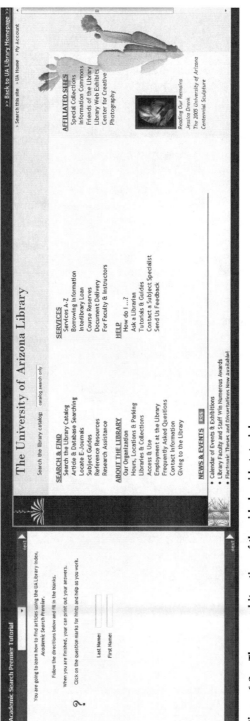

Figure 6.2. The second iteration of the side-by-side tutorials.

When students completed the tutorial, the instructors reviewed them and provided individual student feedback to the extent necessary. In situations where the preassessment revealed weaknesses in library skills shared by the class as a whole, the instructors coordinated with designated librarians who were available to provide in-class instruction tailored to the group's specifically identified needs. Because the need for a librarian to respond by e-mail to each student was mitigated by the students' ability to print their completed tutorial and review it with their instructors, this method significantly streamlined librarian support for those using the side-by-side tutorials in English composition classes. The benefits of this change were not as broad or long-lasting as was originally hoped, however, since a high degree of librarian involvement was still required when new English composition instructors came on board, something that occurred frequently since most instructors are graduate students in the university's English department. Moreover, librarians who were using the side-by-side tutorial format outside of the English composition program still had to provide the same level of individual student support that inspired the initial change in approach.

Since addressing the time costs associated with the pedagogical approach to the tutorials remained challenging, the UAL began exploring the possibility of having librarians actually create or modify the tutorials without the support of a programmer, as another means of saving time as well as speeding up the development cycle. To do this, librarians needed to learn basic php programming and editing. While this approach would allow php-trained librarians to make quick edits to existing tutorials, as well as reduce the workload for the UAL's programming team, it ultimately proved impractical. Specifically, only one UAL instructional librarian attempted to learn php and never became fully proficient. This librarian therefore became solely responsible for creating and editing the side-by-side tutorials, a task that could not reasonably done by just one person. Substantial support from the programming staff was therefore still required. Given the considerable librarian and technical capital required to support the side-by-side tutorials at this point in their evolution, they remained an adjunct to in-class instruction and were generally regarded as somewhat more challenging to make and maintain than the tutorials that were developed using Flash editing and screencasting software.

SCALING THE INSTRUCTIONAL MODEL: UAL'S RESPONSE TO DECREASING BUDGETS AND PERSONNEL

The years leading up to 2005 saw a number of budget cuts at the university as well as the university library. Given the scope of these cuts, the UAL lost a significant number of librarians and staff. This loss meant that there were far fewer librarians available to teach traditional in-class sessions and fewer staff to help with programming needs. Since these cuts were coupled with the university's expanding student enrollment, the UAL was under considerable pressure to find methods to support student learning that did not require direct, librarian-led instruction.

While moving away from direct instruction was a clear departure from the instructional methods utilized by the UAL for decades, this new approach had several clear advantages. From a management perspective, a useful alternative to the one-shot information literacy class would save significant staff time and allow the UAL to divert its increasingly limited resources to other critical projects. From an instructional perspective, moving instruction online would give students unprecedented full-time access to library support services. The problem, of course, was developing a tool that offered a level of support comparable to that traditionally provided directly from librarians.

At first blush, the side-by-side tutorial was the ideal candidate for this new tool. It was already an integral part of many courses offered by the university and was beginning to be used by many instructors as the primary, if not exclusive, means of providing library research instruction. The problem, however, continued to be the amount of time it took librarians and programming staff to prepare and maintain each tutorial. Indeed, one internal estimate logged the development, programming, editing, and grading time for 200 students at approximately 120 hours per new tutorial. Once created, the time required to maintain and update the tutorial was found to be about 40 total hours of librarian and programming staff time. There was also the matter of providing individual student feedback, the time for which could never be accurately measured since it depended entirely on the skill level of the students involved and the complexity of the topic. For the side-by-side tutorials to succeed at providing meaningful scaled instruction on a wider basis, a way had to be devised to create and maintain them much more quickly and with far less effort.

An initial step in this regard involved modifying the format somewhat by incorporating multiple-choice, as opposed to open-ended, questions to help guide students through the tutorial (Figure 6.3). To complete the new tutorial, students would answer multiple-choice questions as they worked their way through the process of citing sources in MLA, APA, or Chicago citation style. When finished, they submitted their work via e-mail to a librarian as well as to their instructor. In this model, the librarian or the instructor was still required to evaluate and respond to each student to let him or her know whether one successfully mastered the concepts being taught, but the multiple-choice questions were far more efficient to answer than the original open-ended questions, so response times were expected to be faster and li-

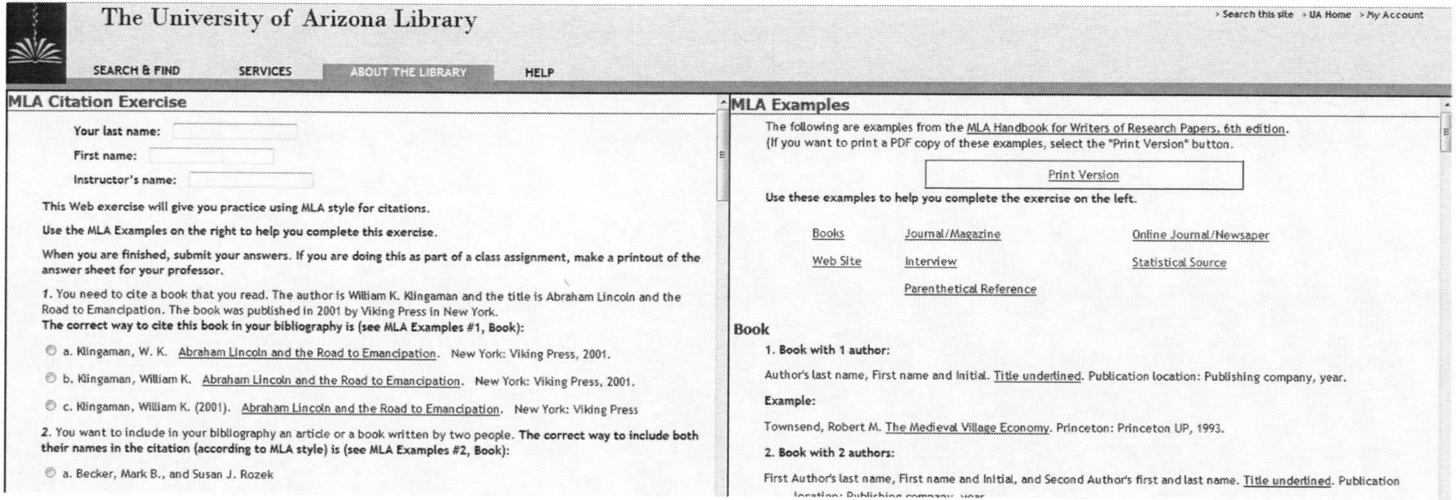

The University of Arizona Library

SEARCH & FIND   SERVICES   ABOUT THE LIBRARY   HELP

MLA Citation Exercise

This Web exercise will give you practice using MLA style for citations.

Your last name: _____

First name: _____

Instructor's name: _____

Use the MLA Examples on the right to help you complete this exercise.

When you are finished, submit your answers. If you are doing this as part of a class assignment, make a printout of the answer sheet for your professor.

1. You need to cite a book that you read. The author is William K. Klingaman and the title is Abraham Lincoln and the Road to Emancipation. The book was published in 2001 by Viking Press in New York.
The correct way to cite this book in your bibliography is (see MLA Examples #1, Book):

○ a. Klingaman, W. K. Abraham Lincoln and the Road to Emancipation. New York: Viking Press, 2001.

○ b. Klingaman, William K. Abraham Lincoln and the Road to Emancipation. New York: Viking Press, 2001.

○ c. Klingaman, William K. (2001). Abraham Lincoln and the Road to Emancipation. New York: Viking Press

2. You want to include in your bibliography an article or a book written by two people. The correct way to include both their names in the citation (according to MLA style) is (see MLA Examples #2, Book):

○ a. Becker, Mark B., and Susan J. Rozek

MLA Examples

The following are examples from the MLA Handbook for Writers of Research Papers, 6th edition. (If you want to print a PDF copy of these examples, select the "Print Version" button.

Print Version

Use these examples to help you complete the exercise on the left.

Books   Journal/Magazine   Online Journal/Newspaper

Web Site   Interview   Statistical Source

               Parenthetical Reference

Book

1. Book with 1 author:

Author's last name, First name and Initial. Title underlined. Publication location: Publishing company, year.

Example:

Townsend, Robert M. The Medieval Village Economy. Princeton: Princeton UP, 1993.

2. Book with 2 authors:

First Author's last name, First name and Initial, and Second Author's first and last name. Title underlined. Publication location: Publishing company, year.

Figure 6.3.   The first iteration of the multiple-choice format.

brarian assessment time would be reduced. This new format was piloted with an undergraduate history class and, based on faculty and student feedback, was deemed to be a great success.

The successful pilot of the multiple-choice format was an encouraging step in the right direction. The next challenge was to find new ways to take advantage of the efficiencies offered by the multiple-choice format while ensuring that the side-by-side tutorials remained pedagogically sound. The UAL also wanted to explore the possibility of using the same tutorial to support a number of learning situations and disciplines. Thought was also given to whether the tool could be used internally to provide reference desk training, among other things.

The desire to scale the format as much as possible required a philosophical shift within the organization and therefore was not without its detractors. UAL librarians, many of whom had long been accustomed and deeply committed to providing direct student support, were concerned that student learning would be diminished if library instruction was to be provided primarily online. Programmers were also concerned that opening up the functionality of one tutorial so that it could be used in multiple uncontrolled and unmonitored situations could lead to a catastrophic security breach. However, after much negotiation and many agreements to closely monitor the pedagogy and security concerns, the first side-by-side tutorial was created that did not require any intervention by a librarian once it was developed and programmed.

This new tutorial used multiple-choice questions with a built-in feedback mechanism to guide students through the process of searching the library catalog (Figure 6.4). To ensure that students learned the concepts in the tutorial, a self-grading, multiple-choice quiz was added at the end. Once the quiz was completed, students could e-mail the quiz and its results to whomever they wished. Feedback from the first pilots revealed that the new tutorials were immensely popular with students and faculty. Students liked that they would get immediate feedback from the multiple-choice questions and that they could complete the tutorial at a time that was convenient for them. Faculty liked that they received valuable assessment data from the quiz, which they did not have to grade themselves. The success of this new tutorial paved the way for the creation of several more that continue to enhance and replace librarian-led, in-class research instruction.

SCALING THE TECHNICAL MODEL

This format remained in use with few modifications until late 2010, when the instructional design librarian and the programmers that had been involved in

Figure 6.4. Fully multiple-choice tutorial with built-in feedback and a self-grading quiz.

developing and supporting the existing model began experimenting with various time-saving measures. Although the instruction offered in the side-by-side format became more efficient with the introduction of multiple-choice questions and self-grading quizzes, creating the tutorials was still a very labor-intensive process. The true measure of scalability could not be reached until that particular hurdle was overcome.

It was realized fairly early on that having one php-trained librarian to program the tutorials was completely unworkable. The instructional librarian and the programmers therefore revisited an earlier idea that involved creating an interface that would allow tutorials to be easily developed and revised by a much larger group of people, including those who may not possess programming skills. If such an interface could be created, anyone within the organization could develop and publish an interactive tutorial independent of the programming staff. This approach could dramatically reduce the involvement of programmers and librarians and thus enable the side-by-side model to become a truly scalable addition to the UAL's instructional offerings. Given its potential, the UAL team working on the project also decided to try to make the administrative interface open source so that, to the extent it proved successful, it could be shared with the library community as a whole.

The first administrative interface was built in 2010–2011 using cakephp. The programmer leading the development of this phase spent approximately 440 hours creating the interface. Although this is a large up-front investment of time, the hours spent allowed the UAL to save approximately 100 programming hours per new tutorial created once the interface was implemented. Upon completion, the programmer, instructional librarian, and the UAL's web designer spent several more hours working together to test the interface and ensure that it was intuitive enough for individuals throughout the library to use with little or no training. Once the initial bugs and design issues were addressed, the software was made available to the rest of the UAL. Librarians were quite enthusiastic about the administrative interface and began building a number of tutorials.

As an indication of the how well received the new development tool was, before the release of the administrative interface (Figure 6.5), the UAL offered only 5 side-by-side tutorials, each of which had been made and maintained by primarily one librarian and programmer. After its release, that number quickly grew to 25 and continues to expand with additions from a much larger group of librarians. From August 23, 2011, to August 23, 2012, the tutorials that have been created received a total of 72,866 uses—47,028 of which have been unique. It would have been nearly impossible for the current team of 10 instructional librarians to support this number of users in the space of a year. By releasing control of the tutorial creation process, the program-

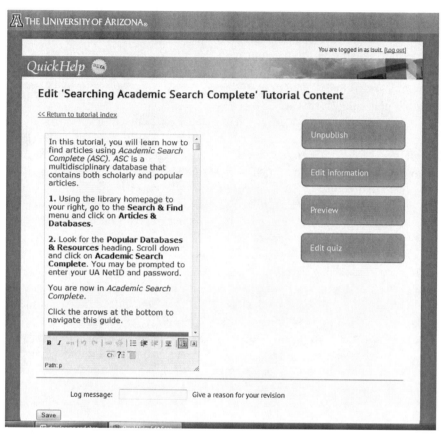

Figure 6.5.   Administrative interface.

ming team also saved itself a tremendous amount of time and frustration and opened the doors to a broad range of librarian creativity. Indeed, within the first month of releasing the administrative interface, librarians started to expand the existing functionality of the software and devised several strategies for improving how instruction is delivered in the side-by-side format.

Along with the development of the administrative interface, the public interface received another major graphic overhaul in 2011. The updated design was based on small-scale usability tests and user feedback. Given what was learned from testing and feedback, the team working on the project enhanced the user experience by developing an interface with improved navigation and a better graphical presentation. Additionally, with this iteration, students now had the ability to send quiz results to multiple e-mail addresses, which was a feature often requested by students and faculty. The final major improvement came when a much more obvious link was placed at the end of each tutorial for users to provide their thoughts and make suggestions. In a somewhat unexpected fashion, the user-feedback mechanism was also significantly improved by adding the following simple question: "What did you think of the tutorial?" Since adding that question, the depth, quality, and quantity of user responses have increased dramatically. Students from a large psychology class have recently shared the following: "This tutorial was extremely informative and helpful. I was unsure about searching for scholarly articles. After viewing this tutorial I do not think I will have a problem locating them for a paper" and "Very helpful worked with PyscINFO before, but gained additional knowledge very quick." Students also let librarians know when things need to be corrected; for example, I received a number of messages similar to this one when some JSTOR search results had changed: "May need to be updated as I was getting more results." The feedback is collected and analyzed regularly. It is used to make immediate fixes as well as inform decisions regarding minor enhancements as well as future overhauls.

Once the administrative interface was in place and the new tutorial format in use on the University of Arizona campus, the team began the process of releasing the code to the rest of the library community. To do this, the team worked with the University of Arizona's Office of Technology Transfer to select a software licensing agreement and come up with a formal name for the tool. After gathering suggestions from library colleagues and students, the team officially named the software the Guide on the Side (Figure 6.6). After completing the licensing agreements, the team constructed a site where users could learn about the tool, join a discussion group, sign up for a demo account, and download the software. The programmer that was responsible for the development of this phase of the tool also posted the software on GitHub. The site was launched on June 29, 2012 (http://code.library.arizona.edu/gots/). Since then, there have 793 unique visitors to the main site and 231 visits to the download area. There are currently 64 members enrolled in the Google discussion group. Members of the Google group actively seek and share troubleshooting advice and share ideas for ways to enhance the software. All of the information is being tracked by the team that developed and released the software and will be used to help guide future enhancements.

THE FUTURE OF THE GUIDE ON THE SIDE

For 2012–2013, the UAL plans on extending the Guide on the Side tutorial interface to allow librarians to construct tutorials that address a student

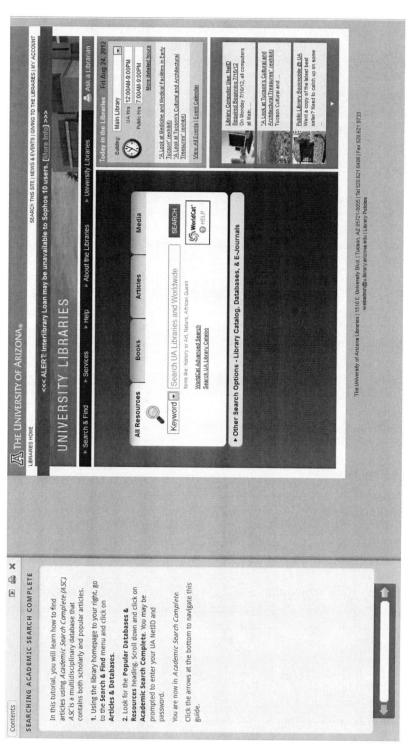

Figure 6.6. The current iteration of the Guide on the Side tutorials.

question at the point of need. These will have more of a "quick help" feel and will not require students to work through an entire process when all they may need to know is how to properly cite an article that they find in a particular database. Most exciting, the UAL is going to explore offering the Guide on the Side as a hosted service to libraries that do not have the programming staff to download, install, and support the tool. This is being explored as a part of the University of Arizona's land grant mission. If hosting is feasible, the service will initially be made available to schools, colleges, and universities within Arizona and then rolled out nationally once the service model is in place. Finally, the UAL will be conducting a research study that will assess a Guide on the Side tutorial against a screencast tutorial to see which format helps students better learn and retain information. The study was completed in November 2012, and results will be released as soon as they are analyzed. Although the initial implementation took a large amount of time, the process of developing and releasing a piece of open source software to support student learning has proven to be an incredible opportunity to learn from colleagues within the UAL and across the United States and to support students where and when they need help.

7

Screencasting for Instruction and Reference

Greg R. Notess
Montana State University Library

Screencasting, recorded videos of screen motion with audio commentary, has become a standard technique for sharing information about new software, creating technology tutorials, and demonstrating online pathways. As libraries buy evermore online resources and make more and more of their collections and services available online, instruction and reference services need to move online to support our online public. With the meteoric rise in popularity of online video, especially at YouTube, and the wide availability of video on computers, laptops, tablets, and smartphones, video-based instruction such as screencasts can be fast and simple to create for an audience used to viewing videos.

In libraries, screencasts are used for instructional tutorials, remote support, and distance education. Reference librarians can use a screencast as an instructional aid for phone or virtual reference services. Jacobsen (2009, 2011) reports creating quick educational screencasts to show a user how to get specific results. In another example, electronic resource librarians can use screencasts for troubleshooting access problems (Hartnett & Thompson, 2010).

For in-person, course-integrated instruction sessions, a screencast can show how off-site access looks even while on campus. A screencast can become a short introduction demonstrating a process to be taught later. Screencasts can be backups for live demonstration when Internet access fails. A looped screencast without audio can be left on the display screen during hands-on class time so that students can see the process repeatedly if they do not get it right the first time.

ORIGIN

Instructional tutorials in libraries have been used for information literacy training for decades, moving from workbooks to handouts to online just as our resources change. The Texas Information Literacy Tutorial (2004) and other web-based tutorials were used by many libraries in the 1990s and early 21st century. In reviewing many of the available tutorials at that time, many were either well-designed ones with good graphics but low-quality content or high-quality content tutorials that were text heavy with little or poor graphic content. The few exceptions were ones that took years to develop and were often group creations with significant investment behind them.

One significant problem with creating extensive online tutorials is that the pace of change in library online resources is very fast. Vendors merge; product names change; search interface design is updated annually or even more frequently. Any library with hundreds of resources could see a change almost every day.

Back in 2005, when I first saw a screencast by Jon Udell, it was an epiphany. Jon's 8-minute screencast demonstrated Wikipedia's history function. While the screencast started slow, once it demonstrated how you could browse from one version of a Wikipedia article to the next, the instructional point was made clear to me. Instead of having a next button with lots of text on the screen (as in older tutorials), I could just watch and listen to the demonstration and could even use the video control buttons to pause or replay a section. More like television than reading, it seemed an effective way to teach concepts.

After first seeing a screencast and reading about the software used to produce one, I downloaded a free 30-day trial of Techsmith's Camtasia Studio. Fortunately, soon after I had learned the basics of the software, I got an e-mail reference question related to a nursing search problem. As I began to respond using text in an e-mail, it occurred to me that this answer (which had about 12 steps to get to the information the student wanted) would be a great opportunity to try using a screencast in a library setting. Even when I was new to the Camtasia and the software was not as easy to use as it is today, it only took about 45 minutes to create a quick tutorial demonstrating all 12 steps. I could then e-mail both textual directions and a link to the video screencast.

Jon's Heavy Metal Umlaut screencast is still online at http://jonudell.net/udell/gems/umlaut/umlaut.html, and it was Jon who decided on the term *screencast* after he ran a "Name That Genre" contest for it (Udell, 2004a). Two people, Deeje Cooley and Joseph McDonald, actually suggested using the name of "screencast" (Udell, 2004b).

OBJECTIVES

After successfully creating one screencast and using it within an instruction and reference environment, I decided to pursue the technology officially at work and look for instructional opportunities for using screencasts for e-learning. While creating a proposal for purchasing the appropriate software and hardware was a first step, the process of determining where screencasting could be most appropriately used for e-learning was a longer process. Several initial objectives occurred to me, including

- support for e-mail and virtual reference,
- quick tutorials for frequently (and infrequently) asked questions, and
- embedding class-specific tutorials in course guides such as LibGuides.

Beyond instructional uses for screencasts, promoting the technology to other reference and instruction librarians and evaluating different hosting options were other primary aims.

The first few screencasts published can help meet the objective of promoting the technology to other librarians. In response to a question about finding videos in the library catalog of the time (which was not a very intuitive process), I created a short 3-minute screencast tutorial. After using it to answer the individual question, I then was able to add it to a newly created tutorials page on the library website. I was pleased to hear from other librarians that it was being used by departments that I had not anticipated; plus, it made other librarians more aware of screencasts and their use for instruction.

In a similar way, I started expanding the number of screencast tutorials to try to meet the needs of frequently asked questions. Especially for those that required a complex series of steps (i.e., anything longer than a few clicks) to achieve the hoped-for search results, a screencast seemed like a natural way to provide such on-demand instruction. In addition, infrequently asked questions with a complex process could work as well. For example, every so often we would get asked about how to find non-English-language books in the catalog. While the advanced-search language limit made this easy, it did not meet most students' needs. The problem was that on a search for French books, for example, many of the results were nonfiction books, often in Canadian government publications that were in both French and English. Most students wanted to find fiction in French. The nonintuitive solution is to use both the language limit on the advanced search page and then the Library of Congress classification facet of "Romance Languages" to get to what students want. It is a nonintuitive-enough strategy that it can be hard to remember for librarians who use the trick relatively infrequently. By creating a screencast, it helps reinforce the approach in the creator's memory, and it provides a screencast instructional tutorial for self-service students and for librarians who remembered that there is a way to achieve the goal but may not remember the details of such an infrequently asked answer.

PROCESS

Our initial investment was for a single copy of the software along with existing server space for hosting. For hardware, a computer microphone or, better yet, a headset with a microphone is also needed in addition to the Internet-connected computer. Back in 2004 when Jon Udell came up with the term *screencasting*, there were relatively few screencasting software choices and few hosting options, and most were commercial and somewhat costly. Today, there are numerous free recording options and free hosting choices, and even the commercial alternatives have improved and offer a wide variety of features.

That can make the choice more complex. While I started with the commercial Camtasia Studio, these days a good choice is to start with the free options. At a minimum, the software should be able to

- record the computer (or tablet) screen,
- simultaneously record an audio track, and
- produce a Flash, HTML5, and/or YouTube video.

Two free online recording choices that come with free hosting as well (and easy uploading to YouTube) are Screenr and Screencast-O-Matic. Both need just a standard web browser (such as Internet Explorer, Firefox, or Google Chrome) and the free Java plug-in. (Java is usually already available, but check by visiting java.com and clicking the "Do I have Java?" link to confirm that the latest version of Java is installed.)

Screenr is a good choice for a first screencast project. It has several advantages:

- It's free.
- Screencasts are limited to 5 minutes (to help you avoid creating a too-lengthy one).
- You can log in with an existing account (Twitter, Google, Facebook, Yahoo!, LinkedIn, or Windows Live ID).
- You can host the finished screencast at Screenr or upload to YouTube.

Screenr was a good choice for creating a quick screencast with instructions on how to set Google Scholar preferences. Our off-campus Google Scholar users do not see our open URL links or citation management links unless they set them in the Google Scholar preferences. I first created a quick click path or story board (at its simplest, a list of URLs and clicks through which I plan to travel for the screencast, along with an outline of what I will say). In this case, I used the following click path:

1. Start on Google Scholar home page.
2. Click Settings.
3. Library Links.
4. Search "montana state."
5. Select "Montana State University—Check MSU Availability."
6. Save.
7. Click Settings.
8. Show Bibliography Manager.
9. Choose option for EndNote.
10. Save.
11. Demonstrate with search on "bozeman."

After running through a quick rehearsal of these steps, I resized the browser window to the smallest size that would still display the important information. In this case, the dimensions 640 ´480 work well. Keeping the dimensions as small as possible helps to focus the learner's eye, keeps the file size smaller, and is a standard YouTube dimension.

I set up one browser (with no settings saved in Google Scholar) and started Screenr in another browser. I check the microphone and the resized browser window, and I scroll the content so that the pertinent information (Google Scholar logo and Settings link) are displayed. I then click the Screenr record button, wait for the 3-second countdown, and then start describing and showing the process. Once I am done, I click the Done button and am prompted for a description of the screencast. After entering the description (limited to 112 characters so that by adding a URL it can fit in a Tweet), I click Publish! and the screencast is available hosted at Screenr, where it can be linked to, shared on Facebook and Twitter, and even embedded in a LibGuide, blog, or other website using the "Get embed code" link.

Adding a new page in my EndNote LibGuide, I embed the screencast on a new Google Scholar Settings page so that any of our EndNote users can learn for themselves how to get to our subscribed content from Google Scholar and download the citations to EndNote or EndNote Web. In LibGuides, I create a new Content Box using the Multimedia box named Embedded Media & Widgets. Then, in the box, I paste the embed code from Screenr using the Edit Media/Widget Code link.

Screencast-O-Matic can be used as well and has a higher time limit for produced screencasts of 15 minutes. For a small investment of $15 year, Screencast-O-Matic can be used with the added advantages of editing tools, advanced record controls, the ability to draw and zoom when recording, and unlimited recording time. For even more extensive screencasting projects, with very advanced editing capabilities, quizzing, and even more advanced features, try Camtasia Studio or Adobe Captivate.

In workshops where I have talked with librarians who have tried many different programs, I have learned that each program has its fans and foes. Given that, I suggest trying several to see which programs best suit your style, preferences, and price range.

RESOURCE INVESTMENT

While screencasting is now easy to do with minimal monetary investment, it does not seem to be a process that most librarians take to naturally. While needed funds are minimal, some hardware and software investments can help encourage more screencast creation. An investment in training can help improve the quality of the screencasts, but the most significant challenge for many of us is that of time.

Although screencasts can be very quick to create, especially for those who start frequently using the software, the planning and execution of a screencast still take more time than showing someone in person. For busy reference and instruction librarians, finding the time to learn the software, figure out the best hosting option, and decide on how to link, embed, or otherwise publicize the screencast can be a significant challenge. Fortunately, screencasts can be quick to create and publish, and for those who invest some time up front in learning the basics, they can find that the screencasts are quicker to create than expected.

Any library staff member, especially any doing instruction, can be taught to make a screencast. To start, find one librarian with an interest and the basic skills. Getting one librarian excited about the online instructional potential of screencasts may well get more people involved. To get more people screencasting, lowering any barriers to entry can make a significant different. Get the commercial software installed on more staff computers, including those at public service desks. For web-based software, verify that staff computers have an up-to-date version of Java installed. Also get library accounts at YouTube, Screencast-O-Matic, and/or Screenr, and then have the user names and passwords remembered by the browser on staff computers.

In terms of funding expenses, the first step is to get the necessary hardware: microphones. While an inexpensive, basic computer microphone can work (even the built-in ones on laptops and tablets), better sound quality comes from headset microphones. They can range in price from $10 to $100 or more, but most library screencasters find that ones in the range of $25 to $50 are quite good. A headset microphone has the advantage of being in a position that leaves the hands free for typing and mousing while keeping a consistent distance between the mouth and the microphone for more even sound.

For creating more extensive tutorials, with tables of contents, quizzes, or interactive features, screencasting software such as Camtasia Studio ($299 or $179 for educational purchases) or Adobe Captivate ($899 or $299 for educational purchases) can be used. Captivate has monthly subscription pricing, and Camtasia has a volume discount for five or more copies.

Training may cost as well, and it may be difficult to have group hands-on training sessions. This is due to the difficulty of finding computer classroom with sufficient microphones. In addition, a hands-on class where everyone is recording at once can make it difficult to hear. As an alternative, small training sessions for a few people or one-on-one sessions work well but require more time of the trainer.

RESPONSE

Given the relatively modest investment needed to get started, screencasting offers an amazing opportunity to provide instructional content to off-site users. For instructional screencasts created for an e-mail reference question, I receive frequent positive comments back from students. Another liaison heard compliments on a screencast for finding videos in the catalog.

In our library, once I started created more screencasts, others became interested in the technology as well. Colleagues created screencasts for use on course guides, with instructions on using databases to answer specific assignments. Another created one for a library course. A third created a series of screencasts demonstrating a bibliographic management program. Some screencasts were embedded in a course or subject guide, while others were just linked from a growing tutorial page.

As more people got interested in screencasting, we got more copies of the software distributed. We also tried hosting some on our own servers, others on Blip.TV or YouTube, and yet others on Screencast.com. Each hosting option seemed to have various advantages and disadvantages. Eventually, we moved to standardize most screencasts and other videos on our own YouTube channel.

For a frequent workshop, on EndNote Web, I had been disappointed in the length of time it took to demonstrate a quick overview of basic functions at the beginning of the workshop. Sometimes the EndNote Web or a database was slow to respond. So I created a screencast of the three basic functions, without any audio, that runs for less than 2.5 minutes (Notess, 2012a). I show this near the beginning of the workshop and can much more quickly demonstrate the basic functions of the software. This helps leave more time for the hands-on portion of the live workshop.

ASSESSMENT

It has been difficult to assess which screencasts have been most effective and to measure the learning from each one. Others have had similar difficulties, although a University of Michigan team reported at the 2011 Association of College and Research Libraries conference that "the results of this study indicate that screencasts facilitate student learning" (Oehrli, Piacentine, Peters, & Nanamaker, 2011). For instructional screencasts created for individuals (e-mail and chat reference), I have received positive feedback from the individuals with whom the screencasts were shared.

We have implemented several efforts to enable viewers to give feedback. Screencasts hosted at YouTube and Screenr and embedded on a LibGuide can receive comments and ratings. However, few screencasts have gotten either comments or ratings. While that is disappointing, most educational videos on social videos sites have a very low percentage of comments or ratings compared to the number of views. It is helpful to see on such sites how many times a screencast has been viewed, even though there is no guarantee that it was watched all the way to the end.

For some screencasts hosted on our own website, we use Google Analytics to track traffic on the page. Some libraries have explored using code within the Flash production to track when a specified action is completed (Betty, 2009). For screencasts created with Camtasia Studio as Flash videos, I have specified an end action to go to a separate page with a "thanks for watching" message and links to the resources being demonstrated. By not linking that page elsewhere on the site, I can just check the analytics for that page to see how many times the video ran all the way to the end.

For screencasts used in a live instruction session, like the EndNote Web workshop discussed previously, standard workshop evaluations can be used. A brief questionnaire can include a question about the effectiveness of the screencast demo. Talking with students afterward about the screencast can help assess its length, speed, and content.

FUTURE CHANGES

As screencasting continues to grow, the software matures, and more of our resources and students move online, there is yet more incentive to continue using screencasts. One new topic under development is an online library tour, with photos and call-outs to make it understandable to an audience in the library on computers without sound or speakers. Another continued effort is to go back and update all the older screencasts to reflect a new website and different database interfaces and improve the pacing and content.

Most screencasts and online videos in general have been delivered online using Adobe Flash. However, in recent years, especially with the rise of iOS devices such as the iPhone and iPad, which do not support Flash, the online videos have been moving to the new underlying delivery technology of HTML5, a standard that iOS devices and most web browsers should support soon. For now, an increasing number of the screencasting tools can create both Flash videos and HTML5 videos, and the best will create both and upload to a hosting site designed to deliver the appropriate version depending on the viewers' hardware.

As screencasters grow in skill, we are likely to see library screencasts that combine the best of instructional videos with screencasts. Already, the webcam option for inserting a video of the creator's talking head is an early version of combining full motion video with screen-recorded video to create even richer instructional videos.

ADVICE

The more screencasts I make, the more I learn about what works best. I continue to try to keep screencasts shorter, smaller, and with as few distractions as possible. In recording screencasts, it is easy to make a longer video than necessary to explain a point. Try recording several versions with an aim to shorten each subsequent screencasts by cutting extraneous comments, screen motions, and less important content. Remember that viewers can always play it again. Instead of offering a comprehensive explanation, try to focus on teaching the basics as simply as possible. Remember that keeping it short will increase the likelihood that a viewer will watch the video all the way to the end. Another advantage of short screencasts is that it will make it faster and easier to update if the content changes.

As with the video length, I try to keep the dimensions small. With more viewers watching videos on tablets and smartphones, the students' screen resolutions may be much smaller than on a laptop or desktop. A smaller video will be easier to fit into a LibGuide box, a blog, or another content management system with limited display space on a page. Smaller video dimensions also result in a smaller file size, which should load more quickly and stream sooner.

In watching many other screencasts, I have found that when I see full screen recordings, I tend to look around the edges, curious about the browser used, the other programs running, and the taskbar icons displayed. For that reason, I try to reduce extraneous visual information on the screen. A smaller recording window that excludes the browser menus and branding and keeps the task bars and ribbons out of view help (as long as the screencast is not trying to show how to use the browser or any of those functions). I have found it advantageous to also shut down all programs not being used. In particular, if I close all e-mail, chat, IM, calendar, Skype, and other such applications, I do not have to worry about visual or sound e-mail alerts, chat pop-ups, meeting reminders, or other unwanted distractions.

Some colleagues have used scripts, while I and others use outlines. Either way, try to sound conversational when recording rather than reading in a stiff and formal manner. If it helps, ask a colleague or friend to sit across the desk from you when recording to help you use an instructional or conversational voice.

I have found that it saves time to carefully check planned examples before recording. As in the Google Scholar settings screencast I created, I can rehearse before recording, but I need to make sure that the settings are back to the default before making the actual screencast. In addition, I find it helpful to look carefully at examples to make sure there are no unexpected and potentially distracting (or embarrassing) results displayed that are not pertinent to the instructional goal.

Screencasting in libraries has become one common e-learning tool. Screencasting software ranges from free to fee with a wide range of features. Hosting options vary widely. The current crop of screencasting tools can make it very quick and easy to create such instructional videos, almost as quickly as demonstrating something in person. While a whole book can cover many more details of how to use screencasting in libraries (Notess, 2012b), simply starting to use some of the tools to create screencasts when the opportunities arise can be a great help in discovering the best way to use screencasting to help teach students in the online world.

REFERENCES

Betty, P. (2009). Assessing homegrown library collections: Using Google Analytics to track use of screencasts and flash-based learning objects. *Journal of Electronic Resources Librarianship, 21*(1), 75–92.

Hartnett, E., & Thompson, C. (2010). From tedious to timely: Screencasting to troubleshoot electronic resource issues. *Journal of Electronic Resources Librarianship*, *22*(3–4), 102–112.

Jacobsen, M. (2009). *Screencasting to an audience of one.* Retrieved from http://tametheweb.com/2009/08/01/screencasting-to-an-audience-of-one/

Jacobsen, M. (2011). Screencasting for an audience of one. *Library Journal*, *136*(1), 142–142.

Notess, G. R. (2012a). *EndNote Web quick demo.* Retrieved from http://www.lib.montana.edu/~notess/enw/

Notess, G. R. (2012b). *Screencasting for libraries: The tech set.* Chicago: ALA TechSource.

Oehrli, J. A., Piacentine, J., Peters, A., & Nanamaker, B. (2011, April). *Do screencasts really work? Assessing student learning through instructional screencasts.* Paper presented at the Association of College and Research Libraries Annual Conference, Philadelphia.

Texas Information Literacy Tutorial. (2004). *TILT—Texas Information Literacy Tutorial.* Retrieved from http://library.utb.edu/tilt/

Udell, J. (2004a). *Name that genre.* Retrieved from http://jonudell.net/udell/2004-11-15-name-that-genre.html

Udell, J. (2004b). *Name that genre: Screencast.* Retrieved from http://jonudell.net/udell/2004-11-17-name-that-genre-screencast.html

8

Promoting Faculty Adoption of E-Learning Solutions and Library Services through Streaming Videos

Coleen Meyers Martin and Lynn D. Lampert

California State University Library, Northridge

When working to promote the adoption of e-learning solutions and digital library services to faculty, librarians would be well served to remember Marshall McLuhan's catchphrase "The medium is the message."[1] Nowadays, the medium is perhaps more powerful than the message in respect to the deployment of online educational programming and digital learning objects within higher education. With the massive popularity of services such as YouTube and Hulu and the notoriety that companies such as Lynda.com and the Khan Academy have achieved, the delivery of digital learning objects via video streaming has become both an expectation and a vital instructional service need within academic libraries. Librarians at California State University, Northridge (CSUN), have recognized these new trends and adopted a combined approach to marketing library services through videos that work to open reluctant faculty members' eyes to the benefits of utilizing video e-learning solutions in their curricula through the deployment of our Message in a Minute streaming video series. Message in a Minute is also emblematic of the online digital learning initiatives being encouraged by the California State University system, the largest 4-year university system in the country. CSUN is one of the California State University system's 23 campuses, and it serves approximately 35,000 students.

LITERATURE REVIEW

The increasing popularity of streaming video within both entertainment and online learning environments has been nothing short of monumental. The growth of the usage of videos as a vehicle to share ideas, entertain, and educate has proven to be a major factor in shifting the way that people approach the Internet and learn about new things. Within higher education settings, the benefits of streaming video are immense both within and outside the classroom. According to a definition provided by Geoffrey Little, streaming video is a technology that allows users to view, share, and download online videos onto their computers, tablets, and other mobile devices, such as smartphones.[2] Kathleen Moore, the author of a 2011 Pew Internet & American Life Project, reports that "71% of online Americans use video-sharing sites such as YouTube and Vimeo, up from 66% a year earlier."[3] The Video Use and Higher Education Project's authors Peter Kaufman and Jen Mohan, who interviewed "57 faculty and librarians from 20 institutions and across 18 academic departments and schools, found that the educational use of video on campus is accelerating rapidly in departments across all disciplines—from arts, humanities, and sciences to professional and vocational curricula."[4] The authors assert that their 2011 study's results show that the usage of video as a medium is expected by faculty, librarians, and administrators to continue to grow at a rapid pace over the next decade.[5]

Certainly, one can look at the success of YouTube and Hulu and see the connection between the popularity that streaming videos enjoy within everyday life on the Internet and students' growing preference to learn from short video clips rather than read long textual directions from static webpages. But the usage of this medium within educational and corporate training settings has other, lesser-known roots. One example of an early leader in the usage of deploying online streaming videos for training and educational needs is Lynda.com. According to Rip Empson, the rapid growth and profits of Lynda.com are remarkable. Lynda.com is a company that delivers segmented online video tutorials "focused on tech content, offering how-to videos on some of the most popular apps from Adobe, Apple, AutoDesk and Microsoft. Lynda.com was a precursor to other companies like Khan Academy, 2tor, ShowMe, UDemy, Udacity, Grickit, Coursera and StraighterLine," which are all now, as Empson posits, "beginning to show how easy it is to flip the educational process—in other words, to use video and advanced web platforms to make learning more affordable and effective."[6]

Streaming video solutions have expanded the possibilities for deploying online teaching and learning opportunities within higher education. Moreover, the ease in which people of all ages can now create and produce their own videos at lower costs than ever and upload them for shared viewing has shifted the average person's role from that of consumer to producer. As Henry Jenkins, celebrated author of *Convergence Culture: Where Old and New Media Collide*, noted in the *Chronicle of Higher Education*, "Try to imagine what would happen if academic departments operated more like YouTube or Wikipedia, allowing for the rapid development of scattered expertise. . . . Let's call this new form of academic unit a YouNiversity."[7] As we can see from the recent initiatives reported by Lewin, MIT and Harvard's moves to offer free online courses via the EdX project[8] reflect the growing demand for new models of learning, the importance of streaming video technologies, and the ease in which they can be deployed.

Effective teaching and learning is no longer just a matter of emphasizing content and promoting sound reading, writing, and (hopefully) critical thinking. The Video Use and Higher Education Project authors describe a "cultural shift today as one from book literacy to screen fluency where video is the new vernacular—'a world beyond words,' where television, movies, and all audiovisual work will, like books, find themselves with tables of contents, indexes and abstracts, rendering them searchable to the minute if not the second."[9]

Despite the literature that purports the promise of using online videos for specific instructional contexts and needs, a large amount of effort is often necessary to convince instructors who rely heavily on face-to-face instruction to consider creating their own video streaming content into even asynchronous learning management sites that hold their course content online.[10] Issues of time, skill sets, and the question of impact are often presented as barriers to adopting this approach versus more traditional methods. The benefits of a library modeling the successes of streaming short instructional videos through an outreach project like Message in a Minute are immense. As Geoffrey Little asserts, "with some planning, forethought, and an investment of time, talent and energy, libraries can use streaming video to create and sustain an innovative and multifaceted outreach program to users in real time and beyond the boundaries of the physical library."[11] This type of programming, when targeted to a faculty audience, helps share awareness of the capacity of streaming video to help distribute learning objects tied to curricular and programmatic goals. Too few libraries have developed consistent streaming media platforms and services to launch online curricular offerings that pinpoint point-of-need instruction or e-learning marketing needs versus entire recordings or podcasts of online course lectures. Short video clips designed to promote one or two single learning outcomes may prove more powerful than earlier-touted, lengthier lecture-capture videos or podcasts that tend to lose audiences' attention.[12] Examples of powerful media and online learning campaigns that libraries have deployed using streaming video through vehicles such as YouTube are mentioned in a helpful 2011 bibliography entitled "Marketing and Promotion of Library Services Using Web 2.0: An Annotated Mediagraphy."[13] The need for digital learning objects that utilize streaming video, capitalizing on its popularity and ease in implementation, presents a unique opportunity for today's academic libraries to promote and educate their user community about products and services and demonstrate how higher education can best approach teaching and sharing information in the digital age.

PROJECT BACKGROUND

Several times a year, members of the CSUN Oviatt Library's outreach committee gather to discuss current and future outreach programming strategies to market and promote the library to the CSUN community. These librarians had been looking for a way to communicate specifically with faculty members to inform them about using new and long-standing library resources. Preexisting and traditional methods of interacting with campus faculty included speaking with them in classrooms, campus meetings, e-mail, and social situations. However, the librarians continued to find that many faculty members were unaware of or underutilized numerous library resources and services. A study by Wakiji and Thomas confirmed these experiences when it found that 50% of faculty members reported that they had learned to use library resources on their own.[14] Since many faculty members are inclined to discover and utilize library services independently, it became even more important for librarians to communicate new and preexisting services to this vital campus community user group.

During the spring of 2010, the librarians determined that drafting a library faculty education campaign through the use of streaming videos promised an electronic and alternative way to connect with this group. In the spirit of keeping the communications brief, they coined the video series Message in a Minute. The librarians had hoped that these brief video communications, sent directly to faculty by e-mail, would provide the new avenue of communication they had been looking for to inform faculty members about how they can utilize library resources. While the idea inspired everyone involved, only some members of the committee were familiar with the technologies that would allow them to develop these videos. Fortunately, the library already owned Camtasia, a software program used to create screencasts, which are digital recordings of computer screens. Screencasts are commonly used to train and teach online; however, the librarians also wanted to include visuals of faculty members within the videos utilizing library resources and services to ensure that they would be able to hold viewer interest. This would require filming actual video and adding this footage to the screencasts. But no one on the committee possessed knowledge of traditional filmmaking. Since it was important that the videos be developed with a high-quality production value and include elements of both screencast and film, the outreach librarian decided to survey their professional departments and communities to determine what, if any, preexisting video production resources would be available to them. In doing so, she discovered that a staff member within the library's music and media department possessed a vast amount of experience developing and producing promotional videos. Also working within his department was a student employee who was enrolled in the CSUN cinema and television department's program. This student was very knowledgeable and adept at filmmaking as well. Also joining the blossoming video production team was the student's immediate supervisor, who had a sharp eye for editing and would help to manage the project within the cinema student's work schedule. With a willing team set in place, the outreach librarian took time to lay out the project's chief aims and objectives prior to submitting the faculty promotional and educational campaign to the library dean's office for approval.

DEVELOPMENT AND PRODUCTION PROCESSES

Developing a campaign to communicate and inform faculty members about utilizing library resources and services through the creation of educational videos promised a new opportunity for interaction between librarians and campus faculty. Yet, the project would require a clear set of objectives to meet its goals. The outreach librarian outlined the following criteria for the project.

Project objective. To produce brief videos from a faculty member's point of view to inform faculty about how they can utilize library resources and services.

Audience. All CSUN faculty members.

Motivation. To inform faculty about the value of utilizing library resources and services and the means in which to access them.

Videos to be developed.

"Course Reserves": To demonstrate to faculty the importance of placing items on reserve and to show how easy it is to do online.

"Librarian Help through Moodle": To show the ease of collaborating with librarians within the university's course management system.

"The Place to Be (Library Tour)": To show where faculty can go within the library to utilize new and existing services.

"Searching Cited References": To demonstrate how to access library online resources for finding citations.

"Interlibrary Loan": To demonstrate the usefulness of the service and its abundance of on loan resources.

"Video Furnace": To introduce faculty to the opportunity of connecting to streaming video within their classrooms through a click of a button.

Frequency and mechanism of delivery. The videos would be e-mailed from the library directly to faculty members each semester. The videos would be released during the most opportune time during each semester but usually at the beginning of the fall and spring semesters. The videos would also be accessible on the Oviatt Library's YouTube channel, at http://www.youtube.com/user/OviattLibrary, and from the library's home page.

Members of the production team. Outreach librarian, two staff members with knowledge of video production and editing, and a CSUN cinema student.

Team roles. The outreach librarian oversees the project, which includes script content and overall production. However, all of the members on the team play key and collaborative roles during the script writing, production, filming, and editing processes. The cinema student serves as the main director and editor, with support from others on the team.

The project gained enthusiastic approval from the library dean's office; however, the library has a modest promotional budget, so funding for the educational video campaign would be minimal. The outreach librarian realized that utilizing preexisting library and campus resources for the project would be essential for the success of the program. Fortunately, the library's music and media department already owned many of the technologies and equipment necessary to develop the videos. The Camtasia software utilized within the project allows the cinema student to include screencasts for the educational segments within the videos. With support from the team, the student director uses a boom microphone, tripod, and JVC high-definition video camera to film the remaining scenes for each production. Sony's Vegas Pro 9 editing suite has been used for postproduction editing, but the library recently purchased Adobe Premiere, since more CSUN cinema students have experience utilizing this program. The library did invest in a Smith-Victor lighting kit to create a professional look for the videos. Once each script is finalized with input from the entire team, which can sometimes be a lengthy process since it is a collaborate effort, Adobe After Effects software has been used to create animatics for storyboarding. An animatic is a moving storyboard for the script. Taking this step in creating a moving storyboard enables the team to visualize the video prior to shooting. This allows for adjustments to be made to scenes if it is determined they are necessary.

The production process is highly involved and requires support from each team member due to the intricacies of the filmmaking process. A production list varies but is created for each video project. The team works together to suggest filming locations, secure equipment, and gather student, faculty, and staff actors. Those on the team also create a production schedule and reserve rooms or locations for shooting specific scenes. Generally, 1 week before each shoot takes place, the team takes time to walk around the library and campus to select shot locations and experiment with shot angles. This helps to keep the shooting schedule on track and to respect the time of the faculty, staff, or students that have volunteered to be filmed in the video.[15]

If student employee auditions are called for within the script, the team consults about possible library student employees who may be willing participants. Team members consider those students that are outgoing and speak articulately. The team consciously chose to use library student employees instead of students from the campus theater department, since team members are familiar with library student employees and can coordinate the shoots with their department supervisors.

The actual filming for the videos involves effort from the team to work together and set up lights as well as clear the background areas of the indoor scenes when necessary. Due to the preparation of selecting shot angles when the filming locations had been selected, each scene usually films as expected, with the exception of on-the-spot ideas that sometimes develop and inspire the student director to shoot more than one angle for a particular scene. Cue cards are often used for the actor's lines, so memorization is not necessary. Finally, one of the team members has a keen ear for annunciation and works closely with the narrators and actors on articulation. Lines are commonly recorded over and over to acquire the most clear and energetic delivery possible.

The editing of the videos is led by the cinema student. With six videos produced thus far and a seventh video ready for release in several weeks, the team has collaborated with three cinema students within the production processes. The cinema students generally join the team in their junior or senior year at the university. This ensures each student who works on the project has at least the basics (and sometimes more) of filmmaking knowledge. After several semesters, when the student graduates, the team brings in a new cinema student to work on the project. This collaboration is win-win—with the cinema student gaining hands-on writing, directing, and production experience and with the library producing educational and promotional videos. For the first several videos produced, the cinema student used Sony's Vegas Pro 9 editing suite for postproduction. But the team found that more and more cinema students possessed experience with Adobe's Premiere, and so the team recently purchased the software for the editing of future videos. Once the cinema student reaches a point within the editing process in which a preliminary rough cut is ready for viewing, the team works to provide critique and input about the nuances within editing, lighting, and even the speed of the narration. Finally, selecting effective background music has at times been a challenge due to current copyright laws. However, royalty-free music that the library owns and music from freeplaymusic.com has been used successfully. The time spent producing each video varies; however, an average production involves 25 to 35 hours per team member. This time estimate includes the hours spent in discussions about script writing, filming, and editing.

Identifying resources and collaborating with other campus staff, faculty, and departments has enabled the team to develop cost-effective videos. A green screen room was utilized to allow for different backgrounds. On several occasions, the campus cinema and television department made the green screen room available for Message in a Minute filming at no charge. In addition, the campus theater department provided the team with a personalized costume fitting when one of the videos required a Western costume for its main character.

RESPONSE TO THE VIDEOS

Initial anecdotal responses to the videos have been overwhelmingly positive. Usually within the first several days of the release of each video, the library receives feedback through e-mail or in person at campus committee meetings about how much faculty members enjoy the videos due to their humor or creativity. On several occasions, the library has received inquiries from faculty as to who produced the videos and what technologies and knowledge are involved, in an effort to determine whether they can duplicate the process and create videos for their own teaching purposes. There are about a dozen "likes" on YouTube for the videos as well. In these instances, the video campaign has been successful in creating more opportunities for faculty members to become aware of how to utilize library resources and services, and it has provided additional opportunities for interaction.

ASSESSMENT

The educational video series' main objectives were to communicate how to utilize specific library resources services to faculty members and to create an additional opportunity for dialogue. An informal voluntary survey was linked to each video on YouTube to gain feedback about the videos. As of the writing of this chapter, these survey results are set to be published in *Reference Services Review*.[16] While not providing definitive results, the information gained from the survey about faculty members' reactions to the videos provides preliminary data. Many people watched the videos, with a total of 3,170 views for all six videos produced as of August 20, 2012. Thirty-one faculty members responded to the surveys. Insights gained provide meaningful feedback for improving the survey process as well as the video communications themselves.

The online tool Survey Monkey was utilized to develop the surveys. The same 10 questions were included within each survey for consistency. Four open-ended questions and six closed-answer questions made up each survey. The surveys were linked at the end of the videos, and those who viewed them were invited to participate at the end of each video that included a survey. The first two videos produced, "Course Reserves" and "Librarian Help through Moodle," did not have surveys linked to them. The team did not include surveys at the end of the videos until after the release of the first two videos. The following provides the breakdown of the views for each video and the responses, if any:

> "Course Reserves": Released September 10, 2010, 813 views, no survey taken.
> "Librarian Help through Moodle": Released January 14, 2011, 744 views, no survey taken.
> "The Place to Be (Library Tour)": Released September 9, 2011, 466 views, 11 survey responses.
> "Searching Cited References": Released October 26, 2011, 377 views, 7 survey responses.
> "Interlibrary Loan": Released February 14, 2012, 327 views, 6 survey responses.
> "Video Furnace": Released April 12, 2012, 443 views, 7 survey responses.

Overall, the surveys established an additional avenue for communication with the library for the 31 faculty members who responded. Due to the modest number of completed surveys, results are summarized rather than broken out by each video. Six survey questions produced quantifiable responses since they were closed questions. Respondents were asked if they had learned any new library information from the video. Twenty-five respondents answered positively, while 6 respondents reported they did not. Faculty members completing the survey were also asked if the video provided them with information that would be useful. Most respondents (26) agreed that it had provided useful information; 4 faculty members answered no, while 1 person skipped the question. The length of the video was "too short" for 1 person and "just right" for 30 respondents. About half of those that responded to the

survey (15) had not seen other Message in a Minute videos, while 16 indicated knowledge that the library had videos on its YouTube channel. Most of
those surveyed (25) reported that they found out about the video through the
link that was sent directly to them, and 2 people found the videos through the
library's YouTube channel. The YouTube icon on the library's home page led
1 person to find the video. Finally, 1 individual discovered the video from a
link that had been forwarded by someone.

The four open-ended questions in the survey provided faculty with the opportunity for descriptive comments. The four questions involved asking them
what they liked about the videos, how videos could be improved, and what
suggestions they had for other video topics. A total of 75 answers were given
for the open-ended questions. Responses were reviewed and categorized by
theme and tone. There were 40 positive comments, 13 negative responses, 16
suggestions, 4 neutral answers, and 2 questions.

Positive themes in the answers to the open-ended questions were associated with the informative and helpfulness of the content of each video. Respondents also liked that the videos were brief, and they reported enjoying
the visuals. Several commented that the videos were funny, while others used
the survey as an opportunity to tell the library they appreciated its services.
Negative themes in the responses surrounded suggestions for improvements
in the production and editing phases of the project. Many other suggestions
were related to faculty preferences for spotlighting specific library services
or resources in future videos.

NEXT STEPS

Since the team plans to continue to develop more Message in a Minute videos, the insights gained from the surveys provide useful feedback for improving both the survey process and the communications themselves. Some of
the suggestions associated with the editing and production of the videos has
supported the team in determining which technologies will be most appropriate to utilize within the project and whether there is expertise within the team
to support using those technologies. A question now asked by the team is
whether it is necessary to create technically challenging scenes for the student
director and editor to effectively communicate the message? Additionally,
the team would like to receive more meaningful feedback from the surveys,
which would involve behavioral questions to be included. It is hoping that
this may provide better information about the impact of the videos. Questions
such as "Due to watching the video, do you think you will use library services
and resources more?" and "Do you see yourself using the library service or

resource highlighted in the video?" These questions would attempt to determine whether the videos have an impact on behavior and possibly support the team in developing more effective video communications.

STARTING AN EDUCATIONAL VIDEO PROJECT

The idea of starting an educational video project can be an exciting endeavor. While the Oviatt Library possessed in-house staff and equipment to support such programming, every organization will have to consider its own available resources. Of course, some level of funding and physical resources are essential for the filmmaking project described within this chapter; however, there are easy-to-use and inexpensive alternatives on the web for creating brief tutorials and communications for libraries without many resources. The most important element for an undertaking of this nature is an interested person or people within the organization who are willing to investigate what is available within their communities and what may be available on the Internet. Here are several suggestions for starting an educational and promotional video project at your library.

- Assess your professional communities for existing video production resources that may be at your disposal; this may include people, equipment, facilities, and funding.
- Consider low-cost (and sometimes free) movie production software on the web, such as Xtranormal (http://www.xtranormal.com) if you do not have staff, knowledge, or equipment for screencast software such as Camtasia or filmmaking capabilities.
- Create a plan that is appropriate for your funding and resources.
- Collaborate with colleagues who may or may not have expertise in the area but are interested and willing to partner with you.
- Be willing to try a new technology and learn from it if it doesn't turn out the way you had hoped.
- Survey your viewer audience for feedback in an effort to improve your communications.

CONCLUSION

Due to the increase in communication through technologies that are readily accessible on the web, people will continue to download, watch, and share online videos utilizing their tablets, personal computers, and smartphones.

To establish a presence within this fast-changing Internet communication landscape, CSUN librarians have met users in this virtual and visual medium, which is preferred by so many. The Message in a Minute video series models how short video clips can communicate specific messages and retain viewer interest through a minimal investment of viewer time and with a capacity to entertain. Virtual programming projects such as this—namely, streaming video communications—serve another and even more meaningful function as well. Such programming supports the promotion of video e-learning solutions within faculty curricula, something that many institutions of higher education are now encouraging. Establishing such patterns of communication and learning are vital for the future of education and for the relevancy of its processes and delivery. However, with a measured amount of investment in personnel for investigation and implementation, libraries of all sizes can develop promotional and educational video communications through a medium that promises to continue to expand exponentially.

NOTES

1. Marshall McLuhan, *Understanding Media: The Extensions of Man* (New York: McGraw-Hill, 1964).

2. Geoffrey Little, "The Revolution Will Be Streamed Online: Academic Libraries and Video," *Journal of Academic Librarianship* 37, no. 1 (2010): 70–72.

3. Kathleen Moore, "71% of Online Adults Now Use Video-Sharing Sites," Pew Internet & American Life Project, July 26, 2011, http://pewinternet.org/Reports/2011/Video-sharing-sites.apx.

4. Peter Kaufman and Jen Mohan, "Video Use and Higher Education: Options for the Future," Intelligent Television, Copyright Clearance Center, and New York University, June 2009, http://library.nyu.edu/about/Video_Use_in_Higher_Education.pdf.

5. Kaufman and Mohan, "Video Use."

6. Rip Empson, "Smart Education: How Lynda.com Hit $70M in Revenue without a Penny from Investors," *Techcrunch* (blog), May 3, 2012, http://techcrunch.com/2012/05/03/lynda-70m/.

7. Henry Jenkins, "From YouTube to YouNiversity," *Chronicle of Higher Education: Chronicle Review* 53, no. 24 (2007): B9–B10, http://go.galegroup.com/ps/i.do?id=GALE%7CA159249039&v=2.1&u=csunorthridge&it=r&p=EAIM&sw=w.

8. Tamar Lewin, "Harvard and M.I.T. Team Up to Offer Free Online Courses," *New York Times*, May 2, 2012, http://www.nytimes.com/2012/05/03/education/harvard-and-mit-team-up-to-offer-free-online-courses.html?_r=2.

9. Kaufman and Mohan, "Video Use."

10. Reima Al-Jarf, "Online Videos for Specific Purposes," *Journal of Educational and Social Research* 2, no. 6 (2012): 17–21, http://www.mcser.org/images/stories/

JESR-Special-Issues/jesr%20vol%202%20no%206%20april%202012.pdf; RuoLan Wang, Karen Mattick, and Elisabeth Dunne, "Medical Students' Perceptions of Video-Linked Lectures and Video-Streaming," *Research in Learning Technology* 18, no. 1 (2010): 19–27, http://eric.ed.gov/PDFS/EJ880178.pdf.

11. Little, "The Revolution Will Be Streamed Online."

12. Lena Paulo Kushnir, Kenneth Berry, Jessica Wyman, Florin Salajan, "Lecture Capture: Good Student Learning or Good Bedtime Story? An Interdisciplinary Assessment of the Use of Podcasts in Higher Education," http://www.pgsimoes.net/Biblioteca/Ed-Media2011-Artigos/11-06-29/paper_3046_33025.doc.

13. Tom Ivie, Ben McKay, Fiona May, Jill Mitchell, Holly Mortimer, and Lizzy Walker, "Marketing and Promotion of Library Services Using Web 2.0: An Annotated Mediagraphy," *The Idaho Librarian: A Publication of the Idaho Library Association* 61, no. 1 (2011), http://www.idaholibraries.org/idlibrarian/index.php/idaho-librarian/article/view/72/185.

14. Eileen Wakiji and Joy Thomas, "MTV to the Rescue: Changing Library Attitudes through Video," *College and Research Libraries* 58, no. 3 (1997): 211–216, http://crl.acrl.org/content/58/3/211.full.pdf.

15. Coleen Meyers Martin, "One-Minute Video: Marketing Your Library to Faculty," *Reference Services Review* 40, no. 4 (2012): 589–600.

16. Martin, "One-Minute Video."

9

E-Learning and Holocaust
Education in a School Library

Margaret Lincoln
Lakeview Schools District

Today's school library is a very different space from the facility where I began my career some 40 years ago with the Lakeview School District in Battle Creek, Michigan. Two full-time librarians, assisted by a library secretary, then served a student population of 1,750. Research assignments were carried out by means of the traditional card catalog and the *Reader's Guide to Periodical Literature.* If a student was lucky, there might be a vertical file folder of preselected articles and newspaper clippings related to the research topic. Ours was decidedly a print-oriented environment where recordings, filmstrips, and transparencies formed the early audio visual collection. I recall the purchase of a microfilm reader printer in 1973 putting us on the cutting edge of 20th-century technology! Yet even in this precomputer age, school libraries were guided by a commitment to service and a responsibility to support the instructional program of the school.

As increased automation and the Internet revolution began to affect library operation, school libraries remained faithful to their mission of ensuring that students and staff were effective users of ideas and information. This mission statement was put forth in *Information Power* by the American Association of School Librarians in 1988, and it can be found again in the association's 2009 publication *Empowering Learners: Guidelines for School Library Programs.* Additionally, the association's *Standards for the 21st-Century Learner* offers a vision for teaching and learning whereby the library assumes a position of educational leadership within the school community. The school library program encourages students to be critical thinkers, to make informed decisions, to share knowledge, and to pursue personal and aesthetic growth.

With this professional support and organizational guidelines, school libraries are successfully transitioning to the technology-rich 21st century. School libraries are becoming 24/7 digital workplaces, adopting Web 2.0 tools such as blogs, wikis, RSS, and social networks (Richardson, 2007). School librarians encourage conversation and reflection rather than the mere acquisition of artifacts and resources (Lankes, 2012). Student inquiry also has expanded possibilities for using the new, readily available online tools. For example, students can collaboratively locate, evaluate, and share relevant web-based resources using a social bookmarking website (Berger, 2010). Most important, Web 2.0 itself has not remained static but has evolved over the past decade, allowing school libraries to leverage the dynamic, social, participatory, and interactive elements of websites to enhance the education of digital learners (Lamb & Johnson, 2012).

School libraries have not only embraced the promise of 21st-century technology advances but are becoming increasingly involved in online or e-learning projects. *Knowledge Quest*, the professional journal of American Association of School Librarians, addressed the new roles that school librarians are assuming in digital learning environments through a series of articles in its September/October issue of 2005. Students will learn well in real and virtual environments if school librarians participate in the design, development, implementation, support, and assessment of learning (Abilock, 2005). According to Rohland-Heinrich and Jensen (2007), school librarians can further serve as facilitators and provide essential pedagogical and technological assistance in the areas of curriculum development, online instruction enhancement, and student learning support in the virtual environment. The role of the embedded librarian is also becoming widespread in the secondary school setting. In this capacity, "Unquiet Librarian" Buffy Hamilton has participated fully in the instructional design, teaching, and assessment of student learning in a Media 21 course. Hamilton (2012) has effectively utilized virtual cloud computing applications to teach key processes and skills, helping students to engage in their learning experiences and evaluate information sources more critically.

My own involvement in e-learning has taken a twofold approach: encompassing information literacy and Holocaust education. Because I entered the library profession several years before the advent of the microcomputer, keeping abreast of technological developments has been vital. I was fortunate to be selected as 1 of 10 cohort members to receive a full fellowship in 2004 for pursuing a distance-independent interdisciplinary PhD in information science from the University of North Texas. This opportunity enabled me to update my skills as a library professional and become versed in the growing field of online education. Cohort members attended several on-site weekend institutes at the university over a 2-year period, returning home to complete coursework. Bonds established among faculty and cohort members were strong and lasting. The University of North Texas model demonstrated that with Internet technology and a variety of educational resources, online learning could take place without concern for constraints of time or space.

Since earning my degree, I have taught online for the School of Library and Information Science at San José State University and in a blended environment at Lakeview High School. Due to a State of Michigan legislative mandate passed in 2006, high school graduates (beginning with the class of 2011) are required to engage in an approved 20-hour online learning experience. This legislation and my belief that school librarians should play a pivotal role in facilitating online learning at the secondary school level prompted me to develop a hybrid online information literacy course at Lakeview High School. My venture into online learning has been shared with other school library media professionals through conference presentations and journal articles (Lincoln, 2008, 2009, 2010).

Not wishing to duplicate material already available, my focus in the present chapter will be directed to a series of e-learning projects undertaken over the past 10 years in support of Holocaust education. On a personal note, I grew up in New York City in the 1950s and 1960s as a Jewish youngster. The Holocaust was absent from the established curriculum when I attended the Ethical Culture Fieldston School, otherwise known for an outstanding college preparatory program. Although Holocaust studies have now become widely accepted, Michigan is not one among a handful of states to require, recommend, or promote the teaching of the Holocaust. As an educator and school librarian, I have been determined to bring knowledge and awareness of this history to the community where I have resided for most of my adult life. A consideration of the following e-learning projects will help explain how my goal is being realized.

U.S. HOLOCAUST MEMORIAL MUSEUM TEACHER FELLOWSHIP

My first formal training in Holocaust education came about in 2002 through participation in the U.S. Holocaust Memorial Museum's (USHMM's) teacher fellowship program. Since 1996, this program has developed a national corps of 275 skilled educators who serve as the core of the museum's efforts to ensure quality Holocaust education in secondary schools. As part of my outreach project for the program, I wrote a W. K. Kellogg Artist in Residence grant to bring the Oskar Schindler traveling exhibition from the USHMM to Battle Creek in 2002. Our community was privileged to also host a visit and address given by Holocaust survivor Nesse Godin in conjunction with the Schindler exhibition.

An e-learning extension of my outreach project involved collaboration with Lakeview High School social studies teacher Scott Durham to develop an online instructional unit focusing on World War II and the Holocaust. Scott's elective course World at War deals with conflicts of the 20th century. We had previously participated in the Library of Congress American Memory Fellowship program where we created a web-based unit on World War I, still available on the library's teacher page.[1]

The online World War II–Holocaust unit that figured into the museum's teacher fellowship project was titled "World War II: Prelude, Conduct, and Aftermath." Various teaching strategies were used: lecture, reading and analysis of primary and secondary source material, video presentation (both of a documentary nature and a Hollywood-produced film), and class discussion.

As part of a final assessment, students developed their own inquiry-based mini–research paper on a Holocaust topic, according to the Big6 information problem-solving model developed by Michael Eisenberg and Robert Berkowitz. Students were encouraged to formulate a research question that

1.   Develop a Research Question

- The question which you choose to investigate will be one that you have selected rather than a question posed by someone else or by an end-of-the chapter textbook review.
- The Holocaust has been called a watershed event, not only in the 20th century, but also in the entire history of humankind. Do not expect that questions raised by this catastrophic event will be simple or easy to answer.
- Due to the complexity of our topic of the Holocaust and Jewish culture and heritage, your question may take on a special format such as one of the following types of questions:

   - Hypothetical questions tend to explore possibilities, test relationships or project a theory. Example: What might have happened if the Allies had bombed German railways leading to the concentration and death camps?
   - Clarification questions sort through various facts and opinions to try to make sense of an issue. Example: How pervasive were anti-Jewish feelings among German citizens? How successful was the Nazi's propaganda assault?
   - Probing questions go below the surface to reach the heart of an issue, searching for insight and meaning. Example: What remnants of hope would a teenage in the Warsaw Ghetto still have held on to?
   - Divergent questions use existing knowledge as a basis to move on to investigate an adjacent topic. Example: Given our understanding of the destructive power of anti-Semitism in the 20th century, should those who attempt to deny the Holocaust be silenced or challenged?
   - Provocative questions challenge conventional wisdom and may promote doubt or skepticism. Example: Should some Nazi war criminals have been spared the death penalty and forced to make amends, perhaps working for the betterment of the Jewish people?
   - The above question formats and others have been proposed by Jamie McKenzie in his Questioning Toolkit model.
   - Additional help with formulating more thoughtful questions is provided by Joyce Valenza in her Question Brainstormer site.

2.   Develop Information Seeking Strategies

- Your research question will be answered through the use of secondary and primary sources. You should use both traditional resources (books, periodicals, audiovisual material) and online material.
- Browse through and examine potential resources listed on Resources Page.
- Note Internet sites that may be relevant and valuable for your research.

3.   Locate and Access Information

- Identify keywords, terms, related concepts, subtopics, additional questions that will help you pursue your research question.
- Consult indexes, table of contents for print materials. Use subject lists or key word searching within electronic resources.
- Keep track of search attempts and strategies by using a log, creating notecards or using the LHS Library Search Record form.

4.   Use Information

- Take notes from secondary sources by paraphrasing or summarizing main ideas. Distinguish facts from opinions.
- Analyze and reflect on information provided by primary sources. Refer to the Document Analysis Guide and the Image Analysis Guide.
- Cite all sources accurately.

5.   Organize and Present Your Findings

- Your task is now to communicate the information and insights which you have discovered in response to your research question.
- You will prepare an essay that includes the following:

   - a title incorporating your research question
   - an introductory paragraph identifying your research question
   - several paragraphs that describe your research in detail
   - a concluding paragraph that expresses how the study of the Holocaust has impacted you as an individual
   - a complete bibliography of sources

6.   Evaluate Your Research

- Your essay will be critiqued by a classmate using the Peer Review form.
- All class members will respond to criticisms and suggestions, rewrite essays where necessary and submit a final product.
- All essays will be incorporated into an in-class publication of "Infrequently Asked Questions About the Holocaust."

Figure 9.1.   Inquiry-based mini–research paper according to the Big 6 model on student page (bit.ly/OU337u).

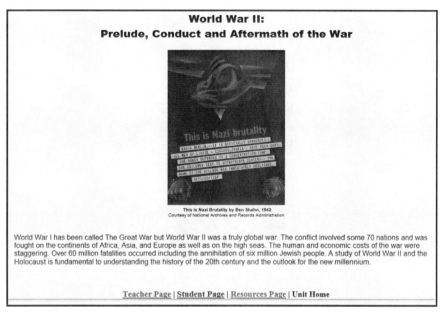

Figure 9.2.   Archived version of World War II–Holocaust unit.

truly interested them, rather than a typical textbook review question (see Figure 9.1).

Students were aided in their research by means of the unit's resources page, which suggested print, audiovisual, and Internet material along with direct links and research help for navigating the USHMM website. A peer-editing section via an online form was included. Finally, student projects were incorporated into an in-house print publication of "Infrequently Asked Questions about the Holocaust." These questions were on display for visitors to examine when attending the Oskar Schindler exhibition. Students from the World at War class also served as exhibition guides after having undertaken a more in-depth study of the Holocaust through the online World War II unit.

Although this online World War II–Holocaust unit is no longer viewable on the local community college server where it was first housed, an archived version can be accessed[2] or seen here (Figure 9.2).

MUSEUM FELLOWSHIP TEACHING RESOURCES WEBSITE

My affiliation with the USHMM and my involvement in Holocaust e-learning continued. I received advanced funding from the museum's teacher fellowship program in 2003 to develop a website that would offer quality, evaluated Holocaust instructional resources and would promote the work of USHMM teacher fellows from 1996 to 2003. The impetus for this project came in part from my work as a 2000 Library of Congress American Memory Fellow (described earlier), where I acquired knowledge of the library's methods of publishing and disseminating online primary source units. Beginning in fall 2003, lesson plans and book reviews were obtained by my contacting approximately 150 museum teacher fellows through the U.S. mail, telephone calls, and e-mail. The submissions were reviewed and edited according to format, content, and repetition. Once again, the local community college web server in Battle Creek provided a test site for the project, which has since been moved to an out-of-state hosting service.[3] The site was first promoted through conference presentations at the American Library Association in June 2004 and at the National Council of Teachers of English Convention in November 2004.

The initial content of the site comprised 36 field-tested lesson plans and accompanying support documents. Lesson plans were organized by categories: prewar life, introduction, Nazism, ghettos, final solution, rescue/resistance, children, literary connections, universal lessons, and global connections. The site also contained 36 book reviews, which were grouped under the following headings: fiction (adult), fiction (young adult), biography/autobiography, history–specialized, holocaust–study and teaching, holocaust–historiography, perpetrators/collaborationists, personal narratives, literature collections, and world issues. The site has since been expanded. For example, a group of reviews of books related to eugenics and medical ethics in support of the USHMM's traveling exhibition Deadly Medicine has been added.

The desire for teacher- and student-friendly standards-aligned Holocaust-related materials and approaches, including materials for special-needs students, helped propel implementation of the project. The resources remain a benefit to teachers who would like to include some Holocaust instruction but are otherwise obligated to meet instructional objectives and prepare students for standardized tests. Despite curricular constraints, my colleagues at Lakeview High School have discovered ways to incorporate these e-learning Holocaust materials into instruction. For example, world language teachers have welcomed the chance to use a poetry-writing lesson whereby students connect history, culture, and language while reflecting on issues related to morality and diversity (see Figure 9.3). The author of this lesson, Dr. Mary Mills, provided a supplemental resource to the current lesson with her translation of a collection of poems written by prisoners held at Theresienstadt and later transferred to Auschwitz. The poems (many unsigned) were discovered by Dr. Mills in the USHMM archives, and they give a revealing insight into the feelings and reactions of their authors to incredibly difficult situations.[4]

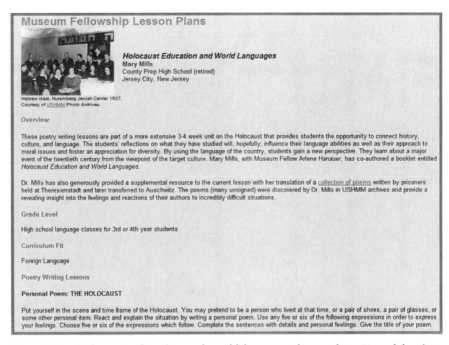

Figure 9.3. Holocaust education and world languages lesson (http://mandelproject. us/Mills.htm).

LIFE IN SHADOWS MUSEUM EXHIBITION

Following the successful Oskar Schindler museum exhibition project, Battle Creek had the opportunity to learn additional lessons from the disastrous events of the mid-20th century through a second USHMM traveling exhibition. In September 2005, the Art Center of Battle Creek was selected as a site for "Life in Shadows: Hidden Children and the Holocaust," an exhibition to be on view at only two other museums in the United States: the Spertus Museum in Chicago and the Museum of Jewish Heritage in New York City. Life in Shadows saw some 8,160 visitors, with 3,800 junior and senior high school students in attendance from all over the state of Michigan during a 10-week period. Supporting cultural events in the Battle Creek community included visits by Pierre Sauvage, Theodore Bikel, Alisa Weilerstein, Miriam Winter, and Rene Lichtman.[5]

To assist teachers in preparing their students to view Life in Shadows, I again utilized the museum's fellowship teaching resources website and added supporting lesson plans contributed by museum teacher fellows and focusing

Table 9.1.   Lessons on the U.S. Holocaust Memorial Museum's Fellowship Teaching Resources Website Supporting "Life in Shadows: Hidden Children and the Holocaust"

Lesson Title	Description
Children in Hiding during the Holocaust (mandelproject.us/Younglove.htm)	Middle school language arts students begin to understand that children survived the Holocaust under varied circumstances and had to grapple with practical issues, such as what items to take into hiding.
In Hiding: A Choiceless Choice of the Holocaust (mandelproject.us/Young2.htm)	High school students analyze, synthesize, and reflect on the reality of life in hiding, from daily activities to coping mechanisms. Students read a first-person account of hiding and write their own response.
"Let Me Sing a Carefree Song Once More": Poetry of Hidden Children (mandelproject.us/Pritchard.htm)	Reading and discussion of four poems about the Holocaust give high school students a different perspective and insight into the experiences of hidden children, in contrast to that provided by diaries and memoirs.
Hidden Children and the Holocaust: A Lesson and Pledge for Action (mandelproject.us/Durham.htm)	U.S. Holocaust Memorial Museum identification cards and the online version of Life in Shadows allow high school students to explore personal accounts of young people during the Holocaust, relating difficult historical circumstances to their lives today.

on hidden children. The lessons (summarized in Table 9.1) were accessible online but contained both web-based and traditional materials.

There was a research component associated with Battle Creek's hosting of the traveling museum exhibition, which was first presented at the Museums and the Web 2006 conference.[6] The USHMM had made available an online version of Life in Shadows on the museum's website.[7] Through the participation of teachers who brought classes to view Life in Shadows at the Art Center of Battle Creek, the informational value of the exhibition in its online and on-site versions was studied. Three scenarios of classroom visits were examined: students who viewed only the online version of Life in Shadows, students who viewed only the on-site version of Life in Shadows, and students who viewed both versions of the exhibition. The research was a part of my doctoral work at the University of North Texas School of Library and Information Science (Lincoln, 2006). The study determined that the use of the online exhibition provided a source of prior orientation and functioned as an advanced organizer for students who subsequently viewed the on-site exhibition. Students who viewed the online exhibition received higher topic assessment scores. Further implications for practice pointed to the advantages of using a website to expose large numbers of students to museum content when a field trip to a physical site was not possible due to constraints of time, money, or geography.

Battle Creek residents took pride in bringing an extraordinary traveling exhibition from the USHMM to the community. The attempt to share the lessons of the Holocaust via a combined traditional and e-learning approach did more than impart knowledge. It inspired an appreciation of our responsibility to protect and care for all those who are targeted by hatred, discrimination, and violence. Students and adults gained a heightened awareness of a most dire period in the history of humankind.

NIGHT BLOG

From creating online lessons and making instructional materials readily available on the museum teacher fellowship program website, we began using emerging Web 2.0 technology at Lakeview High School during the 2005–2006 school year in support of Holocaust e-learning. Our first Holocaust weblog, or blog, project brought together two English language arts classes that normally would have been separated by some 720 miles. Students from Cold Spring Harbor High School, New York, and their teacher Honey Kern participated in an online blog for Elie Wiesel's memoir *Night* along with students at Lakeview High School and their teacher Carol Terburg. As Lakeview High School librarian, I set up and monitored the blog.[8]

A classroom blog was recognized as a valuable teaching tool with the potential to engage every student in the writing process, foster collaboration, and allow students to reflect on their writing and react to that of others. The opportunity to publish online was seen as a powerful motivator for students because it gave them a voice, an audience, and the chance to get immediate feedback. For the *Night* blog, historical and literary "prompts" were agreed on by the teachers. Some of the topics included dehumanization, a memorable quotation, and spiritual resistance and faith. Additional links allowed students and teachers to do research related to Wiesel's life and work.

At the conclusion of this collaboration, students in both schools exchanged class photos; they wrote articles for their high school newspapers; the "Great Blog" was published in *An End to Intolerance*, the online global magazine of Cold Spring Harbor's Holocaust/Genocide Project, founded by Honey Kern.[9]

Elie Wiesel wrote letters to the students and teachers to congratulate them on their fine work together.

A presentation about the *Night* blog at the National Council of Teachers of English convention in November 2007 resulted in a new round of blogging, bringing in Columbia Falls (Montana) High School as a participant. While the organization of posts on the blog remained the same, a supplemental feature included an Unanswered Questions section (similar to Ask the Expert). Additionally, at the conclusion of the reading of *Night* during a spring 2008 blog session, Lakeview students were privileged to hear Michigan-based Holocaust survivor and artist Dr. Miriam Brysk give a moving and informative presentation. Students shared with Miriam some of their own writings and reflections, which were then published on the *Night* blog[10] and are displayed in Figure 9.4. Once again, through a blend of online and more traditional instruction, students were prompted to think more deeply about the consequences of indifference to the plight of others and to always question how such a tragic period in human history came to happen.

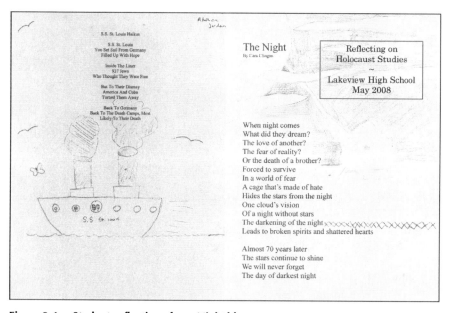

Figure 9.4.   Student reflections from *Night* blog.

GERDA WEISSMANN KLEIN

A subsequent Holocaust blogging project during the 2006–2007 school year centered on Holocaust survivor and author Gerda Weissmann Klein. This remarkable woman (recipient of the 2010 Presidential Medal of Freedom) spoke at Battle Creek's W. K. Kellogg Auditorium on April 16, 2007, corresponding to Holocaust Remembrance Day. Lakeview High School students in Scott Durham's World at War class read Klein's memoir *All but My Life*. They were joined in a cross-generational blog discussion by two other area high school classes and by senior citizens from a lifelong learning program at the local community college.

For this blogging round, discussion topics focused on historical relevance, life and religion, the power of good, the power of evil, family and friendship, and individual characters. My USHMM teacher fellow colleagues Bill Younglove and Darryle Clott (situated, respectively, in California and Wisconsin) moderated the Unanswered Questions as illustrated in Figure 9.5. Lakeview students also participated in an Internet 2 interactive video conference with Gerda Klein, organized by the University of Pennsylvania's MAGPI. Klein challenged students to engage in service learning projects to combat social ills in the community. Students were inspired by Gerda Klein to "stand up" today to the same type of discrimination and extremism that befell European Jews. Our Lakeview students responded by helping build houses for Habitat for Humanity, volunteering at the local veterans hospital, and even collecting school supplies for Iraqi children.

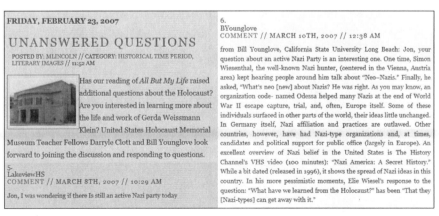

Figure 9.5. Unanswered Questions on Gerda Klein blog (http://mlincoln.lishost. org/?p=38).

The Klein project (blending online and real-world components) was successful on many levels. Over 3,400 requests statewide were received for Michigan students to attend Klein's April address at the W. K. Kellogg Auditorium (seating capacity, 1,900). Fortunately, Merit Network in Ann Arbor made an Internet/Internet2 broadcast stream available free of charge to schools unable to attend, archiving the webcast.[11]

Klein's presentation gave thousands the opportunity to personally meet one of the last eyewitnesses to a horrifying historical period. Her message did not evoke images of suffering and death and was less about understanding complexities of World War II. She spoke about survival, living life to the fullest, and working toward the betterment of all people. We are grateful for Scott Durham's video summary of Gerda Klein's visit to Battle Creek, a true gift to our community.[12]

HOLOCAUST STUDIES AND ONLINE COURSE SYSTEMS

The most recent venture into e-learning and Holocaust studies at Lakeview High School (undertaken with my colleague Scott Durham) has utilized the online course management system of Moodle, an open-source course management system with registered sites worldwide.[13] We have thus been part of a current national growth pattern as reported by the Evergreen Group in the 2011 edition of *Keeping Pace with K–12 Online Learning: An Annual Review of Policy and Practice*. Online and blended learning opportunities exist for at least some students in all 50 states plus the District of Columbia. Additionally, we are preparing students for the demands that they will encounter in higher education, the workplace, and personal lifelong learning.

The first Moodle-based Holocaust unit transposed the content of one of the lessons originally created to support the USHMM traveling exhibition *Life in Shadows* in 2005 (see Table 9.1, p. 112). "Hidden Children and the Holocaust: A Lesson and Pledge for Action" was updated for access in 2011 via an e-learning platform that enhances the online learning experience for students. The unit (accepted for publication on the MILearns Online Portal) is available not only to Lakeview students but to schools throughout Michigan and the United States for preview and download.[14] The unit consists of three lessons, which are accessible from the home page (Figure 9.6) and which support specific instructional goals and objectives. Students begin developing skills to navigate a virtual course site containing such features as a discussion forum, assignment uploader, RSS feeds, and "Ask a Librarian" support. Most important, a real-world opportunity exists for students to personalize their learning about the Holocaust. The lesson concludes with students develop-

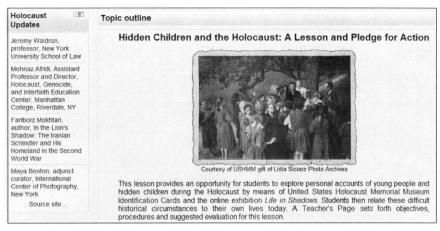

Figure 9.6.   Hidden Children and the Holocaust online unit on Moodle.

ing an action plan and making a pledge that they will in fact do something to make the world a better place.

Building on this favorable experience of using Moodle to support Holocaust instruction, Scott Durham and I launched a second, related unit customized for the iPad. We again targeted the World at War class and developed a unit whereby students would consider the theme of bystanders, resistance, and perpetrators in the Holocaust. Instruction would not be delivered in a traditional way, by means of lecture, note taking, and completion of worksheets. Instead, students would follow a three-part series of self-guided lessons, drawing on the art of Holocaust survivor Dr. Miriam Brysk as points of connection along the way. Miriam, who resides in Ann Arbor, Michigan, had generously supplied high-resolution images of her work and explanatory historical text. The iPad would allow students to analyze these artworks and other primary source documents in much greater detail, utilizing the "pinch" feature, zooming in and out and scanning to any part of an image. Figure 9.7 provides a screenshot of the home Moodle page for the unit "Holocaust Art & Remembrance."

Upon completion of the designated three Moodle-based lessons on the iPad, students would contribute their own "chapter" to an eBook. In this personalized final product, students would link photographs and images from their own lives to the art of Miriam Brysk, connecting the lessons of the Holocaust to the world today. A final class discussion would let students meet and interact virtually with Miriam Brysk by means of Skype or an alternate application. A learning cycle that is truly natural, meaningful, and purposeful would thus be completed.

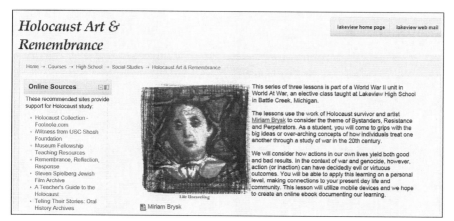

Online Sources

These recommended sites provide support for Holocaust study:

- Holocaust Collection - Footnote.com
- iWitness from USC Shosh Foundation
- Museum Fellowship Teaching Resources
- Remembrance, Reflection, Response
- Steven Spielberg Jewish Film Archive
- A Teacher's Guide to the Holocaust
- Telling Their Stories: Oral History Archives

This series of three lessons is part of a World War II unit in World At War, an elective class taught at Lakeview High School in Battle Creek, Michigan.

The lessons use the work of Holocaust survivor and artist Miriam Brysk to consider the theme of Bystanders, Resistance and Perpetrators. As a student, you will come to grips with the big ideas or over-arching concepts of how individuals treat one another through a study of war in the 20th century.

We will consider how actions in our own lives yield both good and bad results. In the context of war and genocide, however, action (or inaction) can have decidedly evil or virtuous outcomes. You will be able to apply this learning on a personal level, making connections to your present day life and community. This lesson will utilize mobile devices and we hope to create an online ebook documenting our learning.

Life Unraveling

Miriam Brysk

Figure 9.7. "Holocaust Art & Remembrance" on Moodle.

cause as a child of a single parent, my mother means alot to me, and I couldn't imagine life without her, let alone someone forcing us aganist our will to seperate, and never seeing her again.

In the picture waiting her turn, I see a mother, and a child huddled together, as the mother and child know that their time together is short, and that pretty soon they will be separated, and possibly never see each other ever again. In the photo you can see the fear and sadness in the faces of the two, which makes you really see how devasting the holocaust was to the families of Jewish descent. I chose this photo, be-

Figure 9.8. Student example in World at War class eBook.

CONCLUSION

We are pleased to report that the Moodle unit was piloted in May 2012 at Lakeview High School using iPads borrowed from the local Calhoun Area Intermediate School District. School administration saw sufficient merit in the project to warrant purchase of our own classroom set of iPads, which will be housed in the high school library for the upcoming school year. The World at War class eBook, titled "A Holocaust Survivor's Impact: How Miriam Brysk's Art Impacted the Students of Lakeview High School," was published on ePub.[15] Students were proud to view their own work in iBook format (Figure 9.8).

After a decade of involvement in Holocaust education, I look forward to continuing to create meaningful e-learning opportunities for students. As a school librarian, I remain committed to opening doors to worlds of knowledge by means of both traditional resources and innovative technology. Through collaboration with colleagues, I welcome the ongoing chance to provide instruction, learning strategies, and practice in using the essential learning skills needed in the 21st century (American Association of School Librarians, 2007).

NOTES

1. http://www.loc.gov/teachers/classroommaterials/lessons/great-war/.
2. http://web.archive.org/web/20061206062200/http://academic.kellogg.cc.mi.us/k12lincolnm/intro.html.
3. http://mandelproject.us.
4. http://mandelproject.us/Millscollection2.pdf.
5. http://www.artcenterofbattlecreek.org/shadows/index.html.
6. http://www.museumsandtheweb.com/mw2006/papers/lincoln/lincoln.html.
7. http://www.ushmm.org/museum/exhibit/online/hiddenchildren/.
8. http://nightwiesel.blogspot.com.
9. http://www.iearn.org.il/hgp/aeti/aeti-2006/3-Schools.PDF.
10. http://nightwiesel.blogspot.com/2008/05/student-reflections-2.html.
11. http://merit.edu/events/archive/specialevents/kleinwebcast/.
12. http://vimeo.com/47365485.
13. http://moodle.org.
14. http://moodle.oakland.k12.mi.us/os/course/view.php?id=1059.
15. http://www.epubbud.com/book.php?g=XGDWCBDE.

REFERENCES

Abilock, D. (2005). Homepage: We're here! Great digital teacher-librarians. *Knowledge Quest, 34*(1), 8–10.

American Association of School Librarians. (1988). *Information power: Guidelines for school library media programs.* Chicago: ALA.

American Association of School Librarians. (2007). *Standards for the 21st-century learner.* Retrieved from http://ala.org/ala/mgrps/divs/aasl/guidelinesandstandards/learningstandards/AASL_LearningStandards.pdf

American Association of School Librarians. (2009). *Empowering learners: Guidelines for school library programs.* Chicago: American Association of School Librarians.

Berger, P. (2010). Student inquiry and Web 2.0. *School Library Monthly, 26*(5), 14–17.

Evergreen Group. (2011). *Keeping pace with K–12 online learning.* Retrieved from http://kpk12.com/cms/wp-content/uploads/KeepingPace2011.pdf

Hamilton, B. J. (2012). Embedded librarianship in a high school library. *Library Technology Reports, 48*(2), 21–26.

Lamb, A., & Johnson, L. (2012). Technology swarms for digital learners. *Teacher Librarian, 39*(5), 67–72.

Lankes, R. D. (2012). Joining the conversation. *Teacher Librarian, 39*(3), 8–12.

Lincoln, M. L. (2006). *The online and onsite Holocaust Museum exhibition as an informational resource: A comparative analysis.* PhD diss., University of North Texas, Denton.

Lincoln, M. (2008, August). *Introduction to information literacy: An online library media course for high school students.* Paper presented at the conference of the International Association of School Librarianship, Berkeley, CA.

Lincoln, M. (2009, November). *Information literacy: An online library media course for high school students.* Presentation given at the American Association of School Librarians' 14th National Conference and Exhibition, Charlotte, NC.

Lincoln, M. (2010). Information evaluation and online coursework. *Knowledge Quest, 38*(3), 28–31.

Richardson, W. (2007). Online-powered school libraries. *District Administration, 43*(1), 62–63.

Rohland-Heinrich, N., & Jensen, B. (2007). Library resources: A critical component to online learning. *Multimedia & Internet@Schools, 14*(2), 8–12.

Index

About the Editors and Contributors

Donald Barclay is the interim university librarian at the University of California, Merced. As a member of the University of California Heads of Public Services All-Campus Group, he played a role in establishing shared digital reference service among the 10 campus libraries of the University of California.

Linda W. Braun is a consultant for Librarians and Educators Online.

Christa Burns is the special projects librarian at the Nebraska Library Commission in Lincoln.

Barbara Carrel is the special projects librarian at the City University of New York Libraries.

Jane Devine is the chief librarian at LaGuardia Community College at the City University of New York Libraries.

Charles Harmon is an executive editor for the Rowman & Littlefield Publishing Group. His background includes work in special, public, and school libraries.

Lynn D. Lampert is chair of reference and instructional services and coordinator of library instruction and information literacy at the Oviatt Library, California State University Library, Northridge.

Margaret Lincoln is a librarian for the Lakeview Schools District in Battle Creek, Michigan.

Ann Matsuuchi is the instructional technology and systems librarian at La-Guardia Community College, at the City University of New York Libraries.

Michael Messina is a reference librarian at the State University of New York's Maritime College. He has also worked as a researcher at the Brooklyn Academy of Music Archives. The former publisher of Applause Theatre & Cinema Books/Limelight Editions, he is a coeditor of *Acts of War: Iraq and Afghanistan in Seven Plays*.

Coleen Meyers Martin is coordinator of outreach services and reference and instruction librarian at the Oviatt Library, California State University Library, Northridge.

Greg R. Notess is the team leader and reference librarian for the Montana State University Library in Bozeman.

Steven Ovadia is associate professor and web services librarian at LaGuardia Community College, at the City University of New York Libraries.

Lauren Pressley is the instructional design librarian at Wake Forest University Library in North Carolina.

Lura Sanborn is the instruction and reference librarian at St. Paul's School in Concord, New Hampshire.

Michael P. Sauers is the technology innovation librarian at the Nebraska Library Commission in Lincoln.

Teal Smith is user communication and instruction librarian at the University of California, Merced. She served as cochair of the University of California Digital Reference Common Interest Group from 2010 to 2012.

Leslie Sult is the associate librarian at the University of Arizona Libraries in Tucson.